POLITICAL TRACTS
1711—1713

A Hue and cry after Dismal;

Being a full and true Account, how a Whig L--d *was taken at* Dunkirk, *in the Habit of a Chimney-sweeper, and carryed before General* Hill.

WE have an old Saying, *That it is better to play at small Game than to stand out :* And it seems, the Whigs practice accordingly, there being nothing so little or so base, that they will not attempt, to recover their Power. On Wednesday Morning the 9th Instant, we are certainly informed, that Collonell K-le-gr-w (who went to France with Generall Hill) walking in Dunkirk Streets met a tall Chimney-Sweeper with his Brooms and Poles, and Bunch of Holly upon his Shoulders, who was followed by another of a shorter Size. The Tall Fellow cry'd in the French Language (which the Collonel understands) Sweep, Sweep; The Collonell thought he knew the Voice, and that the Tone of it was like one of your fine Speakers. This made him follow the Chimney-Sweeper, and examine nicely his Shape and Countenance. Besides, he conceived also that the Chimney-Sweeper's Man was not altogether unknown to him, so the Collonel went to wait on the Generall who is Governor of Dunkirk for Her Majesty, and told his Honor, that he had a strong Suspicion that he had seen Dismal in the Streets of Dunkirk. (Now you must know, that our Courtiers call a certain great Whig L——d by the Name of Dismal; belike, by reason of his Dark and Dismal Coutenance). That is impossible sure, said the Governor. I am confident of it said the Collonel ; nay, and what is more, the Fellow that followed him was Mr Squash, tho' the Master was as black as his Man ; and if your Honor pleases, I will bring them both to you immediately, for I observed the House they went in. So, away went the Collonel with a File of Musquiteers, and found them both in an Ale-house, that was kept by a Dutch-man. He could see nothing of the Master, but a Leg upon each Stobb, the rest of the Body being out of sight, the Collonel ordered him to come down, which he did, with a great heap of Soot after him. Master and Man were immediately conducted through the Town, with a great Mob at their Heels to the Governor's Castle, where his Honor was sitting in a Chair with his English and French Nobles about him. The Governor with a stern Countenance asked the tall Man who he was! He answered he was a Savoyard, (for beyond Sea, all the Chimney-Sweepers come from Savoy, a great Town in Italy) and he spoke a sort of Gibberish like broken French. But the French Mounseers that were by, assured the Governor, he could be no French-man, no nor Savoyard neither. So then the Governor spoke to him in English, said there was Witnesses ready to prove, that under pretence of sweeping Chimnyes cheaper than other People, he endeavored to persuade the Townsfolks not to let the English come into the Town, and how as that he should say, that the English would cut all the French-mens Throats, and that his Honor believed he was no Chimny-Sweeper (though that was too good a Trade for him) but some Whiggish English Traitor. The Governor then gave Command, that both of them should be washed in his Presence by two of his Guards. And first they began with the Man, and spent a whole Pail full of Water in vain : Then they used Soap and Suds, but all to no Purpose ; at last they found he was a Black-a-more, and that they had been acting the Labor-in-vain. Then the Collonel whispered the Governor, your Honor may planly see that this is Squash. (Now you must know, that Squash is the Name of a Blacka-more that waits upon the L——d whom the Courtiers call Dismal). Then with a fresh Pail they began to wash the Master ; but for a while, all their Scrubbing did no good ; so that they thought he was a Black-amoor too. At last they perceived some dawning of a dark sallow Brown ; and the Governor immediately knew it was the L——d Dismal, which the other, after some shuffling Excuses, confessed. The Governor then said, I am sorry to see your L——dship in such a Condition, but you are Her Majesty's Prisoner, and I will send you immediately to England, where the Queen my Liege may dispose of you according to Her Royal Pleasure. Then his Honor ordered new Cloaths to be made both for Master and Man, and sent them on Shipboard : From whence in a few Hours they landed in England.

It is observed, that the L——d's Face, which at best is very Black and Swarthy, hath been much darker ever since, and all the Beauty-washes he uses, it is thought will never be able to restore it. Which wise Men reckon to be a just Judgment on him for his late Apostacy.

London, Printed in the Year, 1712.

JONATHAN SWIFT, *1667-1745*

POLITICAL TRACTS
1711—1713

Edited by Herbert Davis

BASIL BLACKWELL · OXFORD
1964

14,179

First published 1951
Reprinted 1964

827.5
S977bp

PRINTED IN GREAT BRITAIN
BY THE COMPTON PRINTING WORKS (LONDON) LTD., LONDON, N.I
FOR BASIL BLACKWELL & MOTT LTD.
AND BOUND BY
THE KEMP HALL BINDERY, OXFORD

The CONTENTS

ILLUSTRATIONS

FACSIMILES OF TITLE-PAGES

The INTRODUCTION

THIS volume contains the political pamphlets and papers which Swift wrote during the period of his most active participation in public affairs in London from September 1711 until April 1713. His task was to defend the new government which was preparing to put an end to the war and to justify the treaty of peace which was finally arranged at Utrecht in the spring of 1713. He had successfully launched the *Examiner* and could now leave it for the most part in other hands while he set to work to report on the state of the war and the need to reduce the burdens which had been assumed by the nation.

Throughout the autumn of 1711 there are frequent references in the *Journal to Stella* to the composition and publication of the first of these papers, *The Conduct of the Allies*. On September 9, he writes from Windsor:

> I shall return to town tomorrow, though I thought to have staid a week, to be at leisure for something I am doing. But I have put it off till next;

and again, on September 29:

> I design to stay here all the next week, to be at leisure by myself, to finish something of weight I have upon my hands, and which must soon be done.

Three weeks later, on October 18, he reports that he has just 'settled some things with a printer' and on October 30, he gives more than a hint of what he is doing:

> I was today in the city concerting some things with a printer, and am to be tomorrow all day busy with Mr. Secretary about the same. I won't tell you now; but the ministers reckon it will do abundance of good, and open the eyes of the nation, who are half bewitched against a Peace. Few of this generation can remember any thing but war and taxes, and they think it is as it should be: whereas 'tis certain we are the most undone people in Europe, as I am afraid I shall make appear beyond all contradiction.

The *Conduct of the Allies* was planned to be ready on the first day of the new session of Parliament and was intended to provide a statement of policy for the Ministry and their friends in the House. Swift had been in close touch with the Ministers and had met the two French representatives who had been brought over secretly to discuss preliminary negotiations. The mood in which he began to write is clearly shown in his account of this meeting, which he reported in the *Journal* on September 28:[1]

> We have already settled all things with France, and very much to the honour and advantage of England; and the queen is in mighty good humour. All this news is a mighty secret; the people in general know that a Peace is forwarding. The Earl of Strafford is to go soon to Holland, and let them know what we have been doing: and then there will be the devil and all to pay; but we'll make them swallow it with a pox.

He had everything ready in good time, as Parliament was prorogued for still another fortnight 'either because the Queen has the gout, or that lord Treasurer is not well, or that they would do something more towards a Peace.' But there were further consultations with the Secretary and with Prior, which produced more alterations and corrections. On November 10 he complains that it is a wearisome business:

> Why; if you must have it out, something is to be published of great moment, and three or four great people are to see that there are no mistakes in point of fact: and 'tis so troublesome to send it among them, and get their corrections, that I am weary as a dog. I dined today with the printer, and was there all the afternoon; and it plagues me, and there's an end, and what would you have?

Ten days later he has given the printer the fifth sheet, but again there were corrections and alterations. Finally on November 24, he writes:

> I have finished my pamphlet today, which has cost me so much time and trouble; it will be published in three or four days, when the Parliament begins sitting. I suppose the Queen is come to

---

[1] See also Letter to Archbishop King, dated Oct. 1, 1711; *Corr.*, i, 289–90.

town, but know nothing, having been in the city finishing and
correcting with the printer.

It was duly published on November 27 and a second edition
was called for after two days. For this edition Harley
suggested one or two small additions. It sold out in five hours
and a third was immediately printed. On December 3, when
that was already half sold, Swift saw Harley again and two final
alterations were made in time for the fourth edition. After that
Swift expressly states that he was not responsible for any of
the later reprints, which were left to the printer. I have
therefore printed from this edition as he finally corrected it.
A fifth edition was issued in smaller print to sell for sixpence,
and of this the unusually large number of four thousand
copies was printed. A month later before the end of January
the sixth edition was sold out, making a total of eleven
thousand, and the printer was preparing a seventh.

This success may have been due in part to the exciting
situation at the beginning of the new year, when the Duke of
Marlborough had been turned out and the new peers created
and introduced into the House of Lords. It was certainly due
also to the publicity it received from those who accepted it
as a statement of the views of the Ministry, and from those who
attacked it so violently in the opposition papers. Parker
the Lord Chief Justice had sent for Morphew, the publisher,
threatened him and tried to discover who was the author of
the *Conduct* and of other papers. In the *Post Boy* it was described
as 'an excellent and unanswerable Piece' containing 'innumer-
able Truths' to anger the Kit-cats; in the *Protestant Post Boy*
it was denounced as 'a solemn Detail of Calumny, from one
End to the other': and the number of answers that appeared
within a short time indicate its importance and the strength
of its appeal to all those who were tired of the war. It was
particularly calculated to convince the Landed Interest that
the war was being unnecessarily prolonged for the benefit of
the new moneyed class and to satisfy the ambition and greed
of the General and his friends. It put the awkward question—
what good were his conquests and his victories if they could
never lead to peace?

These arguments had to be answered; and replies appeared almost at once. The first is referred to by Swift in the post-script to his fourth edition; it was entitled *An Answer to the Conduct of the Allies*. It was a long dull tract, giving detailed discussion of the various possibilities throughout the campaign and showing that Marlborough had always been right in his decisions and that the Dutch had not failed to keep their engagements. The second, which had an alternative title, *Remarks on the Tories New Idol*, accuses the writer of 'a Design to blacken the Confederates, in order to prepare our People to swallow down a Notion . . . to make a *Separate Peace*.' Another, *Remarks on a False, Scandalous and Seditious Libel* etc. is more directly levelled at Swift:

> The Spirit, the Language, the Honesty and Assurance of the *Examiner* are everywhere to be met with . . . the Prophaneness, which no Writer has lately err'd more in than himself, except it be the Religious Author of the *Tale of a Tub*.

Attacks continued in the newspapers and on January 19 the *Protestant Post-Boy* again singles out Swift among the 'Calumniators of the General':

> One abandon'd Wretch, from a Despair of raising his Figure in his *Profession* amongst the Men of Distinction of one Side, fraught with Revenge and the Gleanings of *Politicks* which he pick'd up in exchange for his constant Buffoonery, and Rehearsing merry *Tales of a Tub*, can best tell what glorious Fruits he has reap'd from his Apostacy, and Brandishing his *Pen*, in Defence of his new Allies, against the D—ke of M——h: It must be a melancholy Reflection to one who has nothing in View but the present Charm of *Profit*, to drudge on in *Renegado's Pay* without Murmuring, and from being the *Buffoon* of One *Party*, become the *Setting Dog* of Another.

Finally an elaborate defence was prepared by Dr. Hare, Marlborough's chaplain, the leading apologist of the war-party. Though he had professed to scorn so prostitute a writer as the *Examiner*,[1] his answer, *The Allies and the Late Ministry Defended against France And the present Friends of France,*

---

[1] See Vol. III of this edition, pp. xxxiii ff.

developed into a long book of four separate parts, not completed until March 20, 1712. In this he goes as far as he dare to accuse Swift of being the author and of standing at the command of his masters with a flood of lies ready for the opening of the Session. He complains of the confused order of the arguments—'not confused by Chance, 'tis the *most proper* for the Nature·of Deceit, and most agreeable to the Genius of the Author, if I am not extremely mistaken in my Guess of him.' He complains of the misleading account of the Grand Alliance, which is 'such a Masterpiece of Cunning, not the Work of a Vulgar Hand, or of a *Swift* Pen'; and insinuates that the writer of this scandalous Libel could easily be discovered, as he evidently had access to Treaty documents which exist only in manuscripts. He protests that there has never before been an instance in the whole history of England where Treaties have been exposed to the public so insolently, while still in force, and 'declared to be weak and foolish Bargains.'

This is the most complete answer to Swift's arguments that has ever been attempted; and it must be admitted that he exposes the absurdity of some of Swift's objections to a nation's borrowing for the purposes of war and also the folly of his attempt to divide the landed and the moneyed interests. He also protests, with reason, that Swift had made no corrections in his later editions of things proved against him, particularly his misleading translation of the 8th Article of the Treaty of Grand Alliance. In his Postscript to the 4th edition of the *Conduct* Swift had scornfully promised to add a paragraph at the end of the Preface in his next edition to answer 'whatever Objections of Moment I can find in any of the Answers'; but we know that he never bothered to add anything again until he came to write his *Remarks on the Barrier Treaty*.[1] Instead, he went on to other things—the *Windsor Prophecy*[2] just before Christmas and *A Letter to the October Club*, which was finished about the middle of January. For on the 18th he writes to Stella:

I have made Ford copy out a small pamphlet, and send it to

---

[1] See below, pp. 95–7. [2] See *Poems*, pp. 145–8.

the press, that I might not be known for author: 'tis *A Letter to the October Club*.[1]

During the spring of 1711 Swift had several times referred in the *Journal* to the October Club and to the difficulties they were causing the Ministry. On February 18, he wrote:

> We are plagued here with an October Club, that is, a set of above a hundred parliament-men of the country, who drink October beer at home, and meet every evening at a tavern near the parliament, to consult affairs, and drive things on to extreams against the Whigs, to call the old ministry to account, and get off five or six heads.

In April he had been invited to dine with them, but had refused. 'It would have been a most improper thing for me to dine there considering my friendship with the Ministry.' He nevertheless discussed with Bolingbroke the objections of the October Club that the Ministry had been too backward in punishing and turning out the Whigs.

Throughout the year a number of pamphlets had appeared about the Club. In *A Dialogue between March and October* it was represented as the haunt of the kind of bigoted Die-hard who boasts 'I hate Learning, I never read anything but the *Post-Boy* and the *Examiner*.' A more elaborate account was given in the *Secret History of the October Club*, which has been attributed to Defoe; its origin is traced back to the 1688 Revolution, when its members though not all non-jurors, were opposed to William and were called Jacobites; later, in the time of the Queen, they were known as High-Fliers, and finally Tackers, because they were for tacking the Occasional Bill. On the other side *The Character and Declaration of the October Club* attempted to clear the Club of these suspicions and claimed that its members were not enemies to the present Establishment, and were ready to uphold Church and Crown and the Protestant Succession. And a Broadside, giving a list of 'those worthy Patriots' who had supported the new ministry with their votes in the House during the session marked the names of all those who were members of the October Club.

---

[1] Advertised as 'This Day Publish'd' in the *Post-Boy*, Jan. 22, 1711–12.

Swift's *Letter to the October Club* was an appeal to its members to remain loyal to Harley in spite of the criticisms levelled against him that he had not turned out all the Whigs and that he had been slow in rewarding the country gentlemen and the Tories for their support. He was addressing a group whom it was necessary to conciliate, and the matter needed delicate handling. He was entirely on the defensive and could not employ his usual methods, which were so successful when he was engaged in exposing absurdities and showing up his opponents. Here it was necessary to use care and subtlety to win over an audience for whom he had little respect, but whom it was essential at the moment to placate as far as possible. And so, for example, he tries to give them the impression that there is shrewd policy in the actions of the Treasurer and to let them into the secret by showing the complications arising from the need to cover up a lack of power by building up the reputation of having it.

> His expecting Friends impute all their Disappointments to some deep Design, or to his Defect of Good-will, and his Enemies are sure to cry up his Excess of Power; . . . A Minister, in this difficult Case, is sometimes forced to preserve his Credit, by forbearing what *is* in his Power, for fear of discovering how far the limits extend of what *is not*; or perhaps for fear of showing an Inclination contrary to that of his Master.[1]

It was important to try and hold together even for a time all those who could be persuaded to support the Ministry and its policy of working for peace.

There is no doubt that Swift's paper served this purpose; but it is not surprising that a week after it came out he reports that 'it does not sell'; and even a little later, when it began to sell, he warns Stella that 'its fame will hardly reach Ireland' where in the meantime there had appeared already three editions of the *Conduct of the Allies*. But this, his most successful pamphlet, which everyone was reading in England and in Ireland, was providing Swift with a greater satisfaction than that of a successful writer; it gave him also a new sense of

[1] See below, p. 79.

power in political action. In February 1712, he boasts that the 'Resolutions printed t'other day in the *Votes* are almost quotations from the *Conduct* and would never have passed if that book had not been written.'

These were the Resolutions of the House of Commons, of February 5, 1712, which charged the Allies with having failed to provide their quotas of troops so that the burden of the war had fallen more and more upon Great Britain. The particular points cited in these eight Resolutions concerning the quotas and subsidies arranged by the Allies, but not observed by the States General or the Emperor or the King of Portugal, had indeed been publicized by Swift in the *Conduct of the Allies*, and thus the House had been well prepared to accept the Report of its Committee. Only one of the Resolutions was put to the vote, and that was carried by a large majority.[1]

The importance of these Resolutions and their effect upon public opinion may be observed by the tone of a popular sheet entitled *Resolutions without Doors upon Resolutions within Doors*, etc., of which the following are sufficient samples:

> *Resolved*, That no Nation, no, not a petty Conquer'd Province, was ever treated with more Contempt, or more infamously Bubbl'd and Abus'd, than *Great Britain* has been by its Al——s, especially the *D*——*H.*
> *Resolved*, That such abominable Corruptions cannot be parallell'd in any History, from the Creation of the World, to this Day.

In February, Swift was kept fully occupied. Besides trifles like the verse satire on Marlborough, *The Fable of Midas*,[2] he was in close consultation with Lewis and with the Treasurer about some objections to the Barrier Treaty, which were to form the subject of another pamphlet, which had to be finished and corrected so that it could be published on Feb. 21st.[3] He reports that 'the Commons have been very

---

[1] See below, pp. 29–39; and cf. *House of Commons Journals*, Feb. 5, 1711–12, xvii, 69f.
[2] See *Poems*, pp. 155–8.
[3] See *Journal to Stella*, Feb. 13–20, 1711–12.

severe on the Barrier Treaty, as you will find by their Votes.
A Whig Member took out the *Conduct of the Allies*, and read
that Passage about the Succession, with great Resentment,
but none seconded him.'

Swift had promised[1] that he would perhaps consider the
Barrier-Treaty 'at a proper Occasion, in a Discourse by it self';
and when *Remarks on the Barrier Treaty* appeared it was stated
on the title-page that it was written by 'the Author of the
Conduct of the Allies,' and was introduced by a Preface, in
which it was described merely as a supplement to that work,
providing the text of some necessary documents. But it had
been carefully timed to provide the public with the text of
those treaty papers which had during the previous week been
laid before the House by her Majesty's command, as well as
the text of the Barrier Treaty, with the Two Separate Articles,
which had been presented to the House on January 29th.
Indeed, the author of *Remarks upon Remarks* is outraged at the
way in which Swift's 'libels' were distributed throughout the
country:

> And his Party find Money somewhere or other to buy his
> Libels by Dozens, and Disperse them about the Country to
> Poyson the Minds of the People too easily impos'd upon by the
> plausible Pretence of a Concern for the Public Interest. I have
> been told they have bundled 'em up with *Briefs* and Fast-Prayers,
> and distributed 'em by *Apparators* gratis to the poorer Vicars
> and Curates.

But while he was attacked on the one hand as a mercenary
writer in the pay of France, whose ultimate object was to bring
in the Pretender, he was also criticized for writing on so
important a subject in a way unworthy of the author of the
Conduct: 'His *Remarks* are not enforc'd and explain'd with that
Vigour and Clearness which are justly expected from that
Author.' It was also objected that there were omissions enough
in that pamphlet to produce a second Part, such as the letters
between Lord Townshend and the Secretaries of State, 'which
shew the Whigs ready to sacrifice our Honour and Trade to

[1] See below, *Conduct of the Allies*, p. 49.

them, in order to insure that the Dutch would continue the war.'[1]

Again there was a more positive answer from Francis Hare, entitled *The Barrier Treaty Vindicated*, which went into three editions. He points out that the Treaty was justified by its main purpose, which was to secure the Protestant Succession and provide a sufficient barrier against the power of France, only possible by a defensive League with the States General.

As soon as the *Remarks* was off his hands Swift was engaged in helping Sir Thomas Hanmer to draw up a 'Representation of the State of the Nation,' which was presented to the House and printed on March 5th. Some of the material was taken from Swift's papers, and there were consultations with the Ministers. How much, if any, of the final draft was actually written by Swift is not clear from his references to it in the *Journal*,[2] but it may be assumed that he had some share in the preparation of the Representation, which he took care later on to include in full in his *History*.[3]

On March 4th he notes in the *Journal*: 'This day has passt very insignificantly; but it is a great Comfort to me now that I can come home and read, and have nothing upon my hands to write.' Apart from a reference to a visit to Lewis 'getting materials for a little Mischief' there are no indications that Swift was in a hurry to undertake any further pamphleteering and during the next two months even the regular entries in the *Journal* were interrupted by a very painful illness.

On May 29th, however, there appeared in the *Examiner* an advertisement: 'On Saturday next will be published *Some Reasons to prove That no Person is obliged by his Principles, as a Whig, to oppose Her Majesty, or her Present Ministry. In a letter to a Whig Lord.*' This was an appeal to the moderate members of the House of Lords to vote with the Government and support the Court and Ministry in matters where their Whig principles were not involved. Swift's personal feelings of

---

[1] *Some Remarks on the Letters Between the L——d T——nd, and Mr Secretary B——e*. In a Letter to the Author of *Remarks* etc. 1712, pp. 4–5.

[2] See *Journal*, March 8, 1711–12.

[3] See Vol. VII of this edition, pp. 80–94.

loyalty to the Treasurer and his own friendships and relationship with men of both parties led him to try and restrain the extremists among the country party as represented by the October Club and to appeal to all those on the Whig side who were afraid of its republican and nonconformist supporters.

The particular occasion for this appeal was the defeat in the House of Lords of the Bill which was passed in the Commons 'for appointing Commissioners to examine the value of all Lands, and other Interests, granted by the Crown since the 13th Day of February, 1688; and upon what Considerations such Grants were made.'[1] This was an instance of the persistent attempt of the House of Lords to weaken the Court and shake the credit of the Ministry in the House of Commons.

Some editors have assumed that Swift had a particular Whig Lord in mind. John Nichols suggested Scarborough, but later refers to a note in the handwriting of Ford that it was Lord Ashburnham, who in 1710 had married Swift's friend, Lady Mary Butler, the younger daughter of the Duke of Ormond. But Swift's appeal is addressed to a Lord of Whig principles and his argument is that without endangering these principles he can yet support the Queen and vote for her present Ministers. Whereas Lord Ashburnham was a Tory who had been seduced by the Whigs for a time, and who it was feared might be won over by them again after the death of his wife which occurred in January, 1713. For Swift mentions a conversation with the Duke of Ormond at that time, when he had 'talked something of Lord Ashburnham, that he was afraid the Whigs would get him again.'[2]

It is true that there are several remarks in the *Letter*, which suggest that it is addressed to a particular person, one who has 'shared no farther in the Favour and Confidence of your Leaders, than barely to be listed of the Party,' one 'upon whom the Crown has never cast any peculiar marks of Favour or

[1] See *Journals of the House of Commons*, May 14, 1712. XVII, 224.
[2] See *Journal*, Jan. 6, 1712-13.

B

Displeasure,' 'of a great patrimonial estate, and under no
Obligations to either side'—and none of these would exclude
Lord Ashburnham. And if there are other remarks which
would hardly fit one who was very rich and the son-in-law of
the Duke of Ormond, it must be remembered that Swift
must have wished his arguments to have a general appeal to
the moderate members of the Upper House. It is a careful piece
of work, and may be regarded as an excellent example in its
tone and in the steady movement of its powerfully reasoned
arguments of the best of Swift's political writing; for he is here
expressing his own moderate view and explaining the attitude
which he had himself adopted, which led him to give his full
and loyal support to the Ministry. It is the best reply to some
of the taunts which were later flung at him by Jeffrey and other
Whig historians. Already at the end of May, 1712 when the
Letter to a Whig Lord appeared Swift seems to have had another
piece of mischief in mind, which he promised would be ready
in a fortnight. It was of a different kind and written in a very
different tone, with the purpose of discrediting and ridiculing
Fleetwood, Bishop of St. Asaph, by addressing to him a
*Letter of Thanks from my Lord W——n . . . In the Name of the
Kit-Cat Club.* The Bishop had just reprinted four of his sermons
in a small volume with a new Preface, in which he had placed
the Revolution Settlement and the Protestant Succession on
such a firm foundation of Christian principles that it was
immediately seized upon by the Whigs as a party pamphlet and
given the widest publicity. It was first reprinted in full in
the *Spectator* for May 21 with this introductory compliment:

> I should be thought not able to read, should I overlook some
> excellent Pieces lately come out. My Lord Bishop of St. Asaph
> has just now published some Sermons, the Preface to which
> seems to me to determine a great Point. He has, like a good Man
> and a good Christian, in Opposition to all the Flattery and base
> Submission of false Friends to Princes, asserted, that Christianity
> left us where it found us as to our civil Rights. The present
> Entertainment shall consist only of a Sentence out of the Post-
> Boy, and the Preface of my Lord of St. Asaph.

The next day it was reprinted again in the *Flying-Post* with even more fervent approbation:

> The Lord Bishop of St. Asaph's Preface to his Four Sermons, lately publish'd, is such an extraordinary Piece, and shews his Lordship to be so true a Friend to the Revolution Settlement and the Protestant Succession, that none who wish well to our Religion and Liberty, can think it amiss to publish it as much as possible: Therefore 'tis thought fit to insert it here, since there's no material Foreign News.

As a result of all this notoriety the matter was brought up in the House of Commons[1] and the Preface was condemned to be burnt in the Palace Yard, Westminster on Thursday, June 12. Among the Grubstreet papers prepared for this occasion *The Speech of John Ketch Esq; at the Burning of a late scandalous and malitious Preface* is indebted to Swift for a borrowing from his *Tale of a Tub*:

> There are many of my Partners, Deputies and Subalterns in the Country, the Badge and Instrument of whose Office is a *Ladder*, which in a late, learned Tract has been prov'd to be an Engin in Oratory, of greater Use to the Publick than a *Pulpit*, and I am very sorry that by several Sermons and their Appurtenances which I have lately perused, there seems to be but too much Truth and Justice in the Reflection; . . .

It was evidently printed by Swift's printer, as it is advertised on the last leaf of *A Letter of Thanks from my Lord Wharton to the Lord Bp of S. Asaph*, the twopenny pamphlet which followed within a few days. In this letter Swift parodies Wharton's profane manner with gusto and at the same time is able to expose all the more unfortunate of the Bishop's rhetorical passages, by selecting them for Wharton's warmest praise. He even tries to divert any sympathy which might have been roused by the mark of honour conferred on him by the House of Commons in ordering his Preface to be burnt by adding this comment: 'I know your Lordship had rather live in a Blaze than be buried in Obscurity.'

Again in the *Examiner* for July 24 he returns to the attack, imitating the methods of the *Spectator* and the *Flying Post* by

[1] See *Journals of the House of Commons*, XVII, 263.

reprinting with extravagant praise an earlier Preface of
Fleetwood's in which he desires to do the Bishop a better
service, by rescuing from oblivion what he had written when
he was still a private clergyman, before he had become a
political Bishop.

> In this excellent Preface, the worthy Author thought fit to
> charge the *Fanaticks* and *Whigs*, upon the Duke of *Glocester*'s
> Death, as People that would *try to make it a Judgment of God upon
> us for our Sins, by turning the Kingdom into a Commonwealth.* . . . It
> seems his Lordship had dreadful Apprehensions of what they
> would *certainly do*, and *begs of God evermore to preserve us from this
> Species*: And surely he was in the right, for that would be, indeed,
> *giving us we know not what*—His Lordship's Enemies *will tell the
> rest with Pleasure!*[1]

Meanwhile in the last weeks of July, before the new stamp
duty was imposed on newspapers and broadsides, Swift was
responsible for a good deal more mischief. In the *Journal* of
August 7th he speaks of these activities:

> Do you know that Grub Street is dead and gone last week?
> . . . I plyed it pretty close the last Fortnight, and publisht at least
> seven penny Papers of my own, besides some of other Peoples.
> But now, every single half Sheet pays a halfpenny to the Queen.

I have still been unable to find all these penny papers. I have
added one in the Appendix, which was reprinted in the
Athenaeum for November 8, 1902, by Mr. H. Lavers-Smith,
who had discovered a copy which he believed to be one of
these lost half-sheets about Dunkirk, and in which he found
'many characteristic marks of Swift's authorship.' It is
entitled *It's out at last: Or, French Correspondence Clear as the Sun.*
It appeared without any author or printer's name, but was
advertised in the *Examiner*, July 3–10, as 'Just Published,'
and therefore is not among those printed strictly within the
last fortnight of July. Mr. Harold Williams[2] doubts whether
the ordinary reader of the time would be able to understand
its subtle irony; but it seems to me that an advertisement in the
Examiner would be a sufficient guide as to how it should be

---

[1] See below, p. 147.
[2] See *Journal to Stella*, Clarendon Press, 1948, p. 554.

interpreted. I have included it as possibly one of those Swift refers to as 'other people's' though there are some reasons for thinking that it might be one of 'his own.'

The chief reason for doubting it is that Swift does not mention it among the other pieces in verse and prose which he refers to in the *Journal* of July 17. He does mention 'An Argument that Dunkirk is not in our Hands' which evidently refers to the penny paper advertised in the *Examiner* of the same date, with the full title: *Dunkirk still in the Hands of the French, being a plain and true Discovery of a most notorious Falshood, invented by Jacobites and Tories, that the Town of Dunkirk was lately delivered to the English.* No copy of this has yet been found. He also mentions 'a Hue and Cry after Dismal,' which is now for the first time included among his collected Works. The frontispiece is a facsimile of the Bodleian copy, which is identical with the other known copy now in the possession of Lord Rothschild. This has been collated with the Bodleian copy of the slightly enlarged version, printed with a revised title— *Dunkirk to be let, Or, A Town ready Furnish'd WITH A Hue and Cry after Dismal.*[1]

The other Grubstreet papers he mentions were in verse.

The lack of restraint with which Swift lets himself go in these last weeks of July, in rejoicing over the occupation of Dunkirk and in making fun of the enemies of the Court party may best be understood if we remember the mood of despondency in which he wrote to the Archbishop of Dublin as late as June 26th,

> But all still continues to lie very loose, and I continue to be very desponding, although the people in affairs laugh at me for it. . . . The soldiers tell me that the Duke of Ormond could not possibly take possession of Dunkirk, since the foreign troops have refused to march, and that the States will not suffer us to go through their towns. . . . If there be any secret in this matter of Dunkirk, it must be in very few hands; and those who most converse with men at the helm, are, I am confident, very much in the dark. . . . We suppose a few days will decide this matter; and I believe your Grace will agree that there was never a more

[1] See Textual Notes, below, p. 210.

nice conjuncture of affairs; however, the Court appears to be very resolute: several changes have been made, and more are daily expected.[1]

This was only a fortnight before the news of the successful occupation, and the appointment of his friend and 'brother' General John Hill, Lady Masham's brother, as governor of Dunkirk. Swift's own relief must have been great; and his satisfaction prompted him to make a little fun for his friends at the expense of their enemies. What better mischief could be imagined than that the Whigs should employ for their traitorous designs in Dunkirk, their tool, the Tory renegade 'Dismal,' the Earl of Nottingham whom Swift had mercilessly lampooned ever since he had shown himself such a danger to the Ministry, when he had ranged a majority against them in the House of Lords, which had forced the Queen to create twelve new peers. The exploit of the saturnine Earl and his blackamoor servant as chimney-sweepers must have appealed to the cruder taste of the town;—and also indeed to the Governor and his staff, for Swift refers to it in a letter a little later, when he gaily suggests that he will come over to Dunkirk for a fortnight's visit, 'only I intend to change my habit, for fear Colonel Killigrew should mistake me for a chimney-sweeper.'

In the *Journal* for July 19th he announces: 'Today there will be another Grub; a Letter from the Pretender to a Whig Ld.' It is dated from S. Germain, July 8, 1712, signed James R. and addressed to my Lord W——. It was designed to fling back at the disaffected Whigs the charge which they had brought against the Tory ministry that they were plotting with France to bring in the Pretender. The *Letter* was in the form of a reply to a protest from my Lord W(harton) to the Pretender, hinting that he was suspected of having dealings with the other party. It contains a number of promises to him and his friends of specific offices and employments and a strong assertion 'upon the Word of a King' that he had never 'held the least Correspondence with any one Person of the Tory Party.'

[1] See *Corr.* i, 329–30.

During the rest of this year Swift published no more political papers[1] except a few items which he caused to be inserted in the newspapers, *The Post Boy* and *The Evening Post*. It would be difficult to prove exactly how much Swift had to do with these newspapers. His opponents constantly coupled his name with the name of Abel Roper and referred to reports they disliked as the work of 'an Able and Swift Pen.' But we may safely accept Swift's own statement in the *Journal*, April 8, 1711 that he had been able to prevent a letter about the Archbishop of Dublin's indiscreet remarks from appearing in the next *Post Boy*; and again, a year later, on March 21, 1712, when he says: 'Roper is my humble Slave.' For during these years he was concerned not only to censor news from Ireland, but also to see that certain items of news in which he was interested were properly reported in these papers. It is possible, for instance, that he may have had something to do with the announcement in *The Post Boy* on August 2, 1711, of the appointment of Mr Benjamin Tooke and Mr John Barber as printers of the London Gazette. He is almost certainly responsible for the report of the death of William Harrison, his own protégé, whom he befriended until the last, as it appeared in *The Post Boy*, Feb. 14–17, 1712–13:

> On Saturday last, William Harrison Esq.; Her Majesty's Secretary at Utrecht, who lately brought over the new Barrier Treaty, died of a Fever, after three Days Sickness, and is very much lamented.

The notice appeared also in the *Evening Post*, but omitting the tiny tribute of the last five words, which hid the violence of a grief, revealed in such an unusual fashion in the entries in the *Journal* from Feb. 12 to Feb. 16, 1712–13.

There can be no question about the items which I have reprinted from the *Post Boy* and the *Evening Post* in this volume;[2] for Swift acknowledges that he was responsible for them. The first of these is the notice of the death of Mrs. Anne Long, which he inserted in *The Post Boy*, Dec. 27, 1711.

---

[1] For his other papers, published in 1712, see Vol. V of this edition.
[2] See Appendix D.

He had received the news of her death at the Vanhomrighs on Christmas Day, and was filled with melancholy at the thought of the misfortunes which had overtaken this once famous beauty and with hatred for her family who had been partly responsible. He does not disguise his feelings in the *Journal*, written that same evening:

> I have ordered a paragraph to be put in the *Post-boy*, giving an account of her death, and making honourable mention of her; which is all I can do to serve her memory: but one reason was spite; for, her brother would fain have her death a secret, to save the charge of bringing her up here to bury her, or going into mourning.

The second item is the account of the Band-Box, sent to the Lord Treasurer, referred to in the *Journal*, Nov. 15th, 1712:

> I believe you have heard the Story of my Escape in opening the Banbox sent to Ld Treasurer, the Prints have told a thousand Lyes of it but at last we gave them a true account of it at length, printed in the Evening: onely I would not suffer them to name me, having been so often named before, & teazed to death with Questions.

I have printed the account as it appeared in *The Evening Post* to which Swift refers; it was copied in *The Post Boy* for the same date, but in a slightly altered form.[1] A good deal of fun was made of Swift for his rescue of the Lord Treasurer from this particular form of infernal machine, which partly consisted of 'two large ink-horns charged with Powder and Ball'; but all interest in this plot quickly gave way before the excitement caused by the news of the duel, resulting in the deaths of the Duke of Hamilton and Lord Mohun, which shocked Swift so much that he calls it 'the most terrible Accident that hath almost ever happened.' This did not prevent him from trying to use the incident to discredit the Whigs, who were accused of employing General Mackartney to arrange the duel, in which he was Lord Mohun's second, and even to make sure of the death of the Duke by stabbing him after he was wounded in

[1] See below, p. 196.

the duel. Swift confesses in the *Journal* of Nov. 17 that he had been responsible for this disreputable journalism:

> I have been drawing up a Paragraph for the Post Boy, to be out to morrow, and as malicious as possible, and very proper for Abel Roper the Printer of it.

Further particulars were promised in the next issue, and a larger paragraph appeared, dated London, Nov. 20. It was even more malicious and not less likely to have come from Swift, including the note which is added for greater effect at the end of the account:

> N.B. This is the 4th Person that my Lord Mohun had the Misfortune to kill. His Lordship's Title is extinct.

I have printed also the Proclamation for apprehending Mackartney with the rewards offered by the Queen and the Duchess of Hamilton. This Proclamation appeared as an *Advertisement* in *The Post Boy*, January 1–3, 1712–13, and was repeated seven times during the following three months.

But, though momentarily interrupted by these disturbances, Swift had been mainly occupied during the last months of 1712 with a task of a very different kind, which he had undertaken at the beginning of August with the knowledge that it would require all his attention and all his energy.[1] This was his *History of the Last Session of Parliament and of the Peace of Utrecht*—to give it the original title, which indicates that he wrote it as a political tract for immediate publication in order to justify the change of Ministry in 1710, and reveal the whole course of the negotiations leading to the Peace. In the *Journal*, on January 18th, however, he complains:

> My large Treatise stands stock still; some think it too dangerous to publish, and would have me print onely what relates to the Peace. I can't tell what I shall do.

In any case it could not be published until the treaties of peace had been signed. And now at the beginning of the year 1713, although the cessation of arms between Great Britain and France had been extended for a further period of four months,

---

[1] See *Journal*, July 19, August 7, etc.

the negotiations at Utrecht continued to be delayed and rumours spread that the 'present Stagnation of Affairs' was due to France, who was beginning to draw back.

In these circumstances Swift undertook to analyse the situation in the *Examiner*, January 16, 1712–13, and to prove that it was not France but the Dutch and the Emperor who were to blame for the delay, still looking about for something else to demand and still unwilling to deal with any government in England except the Whigs. But Swift was himself uneasy at the slowness of the negotiations and he tries to hide his own uncertainty beneath a brave show of confidence as he taunts the Whigs for their folly in persisting with the struggle even when they know they have been beaten. They may try to 'solace themselves with the visionary hopes of coming mischief' but

> Their Tyranny is at an end, and their Ruin very near; I can only advise them to become their Fall, like *Caesar*, and *Die with Decency*.

I think Swift may have regretted this last rhetorical flourish. The phrase was picked up in the Whig newspapers, and for weeks it was rung as a sort of warning 'to all Housekeepers, and others who are Protestants' to be on their guard against the execution of his threats.[1]

On February 2, 1712–13, he wrote another *Examiner*, which was concerned with a private scandal referred to in the *Journal*, January 26:

> My Friend Mr. Lewis has had a Lye spread on him by the mistake of a Man who went to another of his name to give him thanks for passing his privy seal to come from France; that tother Lewis spread about that the Man brought him thanks from Ld Perth, & Ld Melfort, (two Lds with the Pretender) for his great Services &c. the Lds will examine that tother Lewis to morrow in Council, and I believe you will hear of it in the Prints, for I will make Abel Roper give a Relation of it.[2]

I have included this short report among Swift's contributions to the newspapers* in the form in which it appeared in *The Post*

[1] See *Flying Post*, Jan. 24; Jan. 29; Feb. 5; Feb. 12.
[2] See Appendix D.

Boy for Jan. 29. It was repeated with some minor changes in
the *Evening Post* of the same date, and in the *London Gazette*
for January 31. The fuller account in the *Examiner* was dictated
to the printer, and afterwards corrected by Erasmus Lewis.[1]

It was no easy task to try and stamp out a bit of scandalous
gossip which was rapidly spreading in spite of the efforts of
gentlemen of both parties to stop it. Swift tries to give weight
to his judgment by the accumulation of his evidence and the
completeness of the investigation, while apologizing for the
style 'made up of Extracts from the Depositions and Assertions
of the several Persons concerned.' Nevertheless, nothing could
be more like him in its directness, nothing less in need of an
apology than the opening sentence of the paper, declaring
at once his purpose, claiming without hesitation the full
attention of the reader:

> I intend this Paper for the Service of a particular Person; but
> herein, I hope, at the same time, to do some Service to the
> Publick.

He did not succeed of course in removing the suspicions of
the Whig papers. On the very next day a long letter appeared
in the *Flying Post*, with a list of ten Queries upon the Business
of Mr. Skelton, 'that neither *The Post Boy*, nor the *Examiner*
would have been willing to publish.' They were all intended
to suggest that Mr. Skelton was closely associated with the
Pretender and had important reasons for conveying his thanks
to the Secretary of the Earl of Dartmouth; and to raise doubts
'whether there has been so much Industry used by the
Examiner, &c., to get the Truth out of Mr. Erasmus Lewis,
as there had been to turn all into Ridicule that has been
attested by Mr. Henry Lewis.'[2]

The final negotiations for the Treaty of Peace continued to
be delayed during February and March, and it was not until
April 3rd that the news reached London that the Peace had
been signed by all the ministers at Utrecht except those of the
Emperor, who were expected to sign in a few days.[3] Parliament had been prorogued until April 9th, so that in her Speech

---

[1] See *Journal*, Feb. 1.   [2] See *Flying Post*, Feb. 3, 1712–13.
[3] See *Journal*, April 3, 1713.

to both Houses of Parliament[1] the Queen could report that the Treaty had been completed. The speech had been prepared a month earlier, for Swift states in the *Journal* on March 8th that the Treasurer had showed it to him and he had corrected it in several places and then had proceeded to pen the 'Vote of Address of Thanks for the Speech.'[2] The Address is printed in its final form from a copy of *The Humble Address* of the Lords to her Majesty, April 11, 1713; but it has been collated with a copy of Swift's original draft, from the Portland MSS, Welbeck Abbey, of which a facsimile is provided here. This shows the correction in the hand of the Earl of Oxford, who had also underlined those sentences which were to be altered or omitted. With greater caution and with a better knowledge of the temper of the House of Lords, he was unwilling even at this moment of triumph to ask them to endorse with such enthusiasm and absence of reservation the final form of a treaty which had been obtained only after much hesitation and delay. Perhaps he was not quite as sure as Swift was that Her Majesty had succeeded in procuring for all her Allies a general peace 'wherein the true Interests and just Pretensions of each are so fully provided for.'

For Swift the signing of the Treaty of Utrecht was the justification of all his efforts, the end for which he had worked in all his political writings in support of the Ministry. In spite of all uncertainties, owing to the state of the Queen's health and the dissensions in the Government, and in spite of the doubts he must have felt about his own still unsettled future, he could yet say at this moment with quiet satisfaction:

> now the great Work is in effect done, and I believe it will appear a most excellent Peace for Europe, particularly for England.[3]

The full story of how it was done and of the characters of the leaders of both parties, as he had observed them during these years, is set forth in the next volume, which contains his *History of the Last Four Years of the Queen.*

---

[1] See Appendix E.   [2] See facsimile facing p. 183.
[3] See *Journal*, April 3, 1713.

We Your Majesty's most dutifull and loyall Subjects the Lords Spirituall and Temporall in Parlmt assembled do with the greatest Joy and Satisfaction return our humblest Thanks to Your Majesty for Your most gracious Speech from the Throne, and for communicating to this House that a Peace is concluded, so honorable to Your Majesty, and safe and advantageous to Four Kingdoms; by which we hope with the Blessing of God, that Your People will in a few Years recover themselves after so long and expensive a War. We likewise beg leave to congratulate with Your Majesty upon the generall Peace you have procured for all Your Allyes, wherein the true Interests and just Pretensions of each are so fully provided for that the Tranquillity and Welfare of Europe will be owing (next to the Divine Providence) to Your Majesty's Wisdom and Goodness. We never had the least doubt, but that Your Majesty who is the greatest Ornament and Protector of the Protestant Religion, would continue to take the wisest Measures for securing the Protestant Succession; towards which

nothing

DRAFT OF ADDRESS TO THE QUEEN
(*By kind permission of the Duke of Portland*)

nothing can be more necessary than
the perfect Harmony there is between
Your Majesty and the House of Hannover
And we do humbly assure Your
Majesty, that as You are pleased to
express Your Dependance (next under
God) upon the Duty and Affection of
Your People, we think our selves bound
by the Strictest Tyes of Religion,
Loyalty, and Gratitude, to make
all Return that can be due from
the most obedient Subjects to the
most indulgent Soveraign.

THE CONDUCT OF
THE ALLIES

THE

CONDUCT

OF THE

ALLIES,

AND OF THE

𝕷𝖆𝖙𝖊 𝕸𝖎𝖓𝖎𝖘𝖙𝖗𝖞,

IN

Beginning and Carrying on

THE

Present War.

𝕿𝖍𝖊 𝕱𝖔𝖚𝖗𝖙𝖍 𝕰𝖉𝖎𝖙𝖎𝖔𝖓, 𝕮𝖔𝖗𝖗𝖊𝖈𝖙𝖊𝖉.

LONDON,

Printed for *John Morphew* near *Stationers-Hall.* 1711.

THE

PREFACE

I Cannot sufficiently admire the Industry of a sort of Men, wholly out of Favour with the Prince and People, and openly professing a separate Interest from the Bulk of the Landed Men, who yet are able to raise, at this Juncture, so great a Clamour against a Peace, without offering one single Reason, but what we find in their Ballads. I lay it down for a Maxim, That no reasonable Person, whether Whig or Tory (*since it is necessary to use those foolish Terms*) can be of Opinion for continuing the War, upon the Foot it now is, unless he be a Gainer by it, or hopes it may occasion some new Turn of Affairs at home, to the Advantage of his Party; or lastly, unless he be very ignorant of the Kingdom's Condition, and by what Means we have been reduced to it. Upon the two first Cases, where Interest is concerned, I have nothing to say: But as to the last, I think it highly necessary, that the Publick should be freely and impartially told what Circumstances they are in, after what Manner they have been treated by those whom they trusted so many Years with the Disposal of their Blood and Treasure, and what the Consequences of this Management are like to be upon themselves and their Posterity.

Those who, either by *Writing* or *Discourse*, have undertaken to defend the Proceedings of the Late Ministry, in the Management of the War, and of the Treaty at Gertruydenburg, have spent time in celebrating the Conduct and Valour of our Leaders and their Troops, in summing up the Victories they have gained, and the Towns they have taken. Then they tell us what high Articles were insisted on by our Ministers and those of the Confederates, and what Pains both were at in persuading France to accept them. But nothing of this can give the least Satisfaction to the just Complaints of the Kingdom. As to the War, our Grievances are, That a greater Load has been laid on Us than was either just or necessary, or than we have been able to bear; that the grossest Impositions have been submitted to for the Advancement of private Wealth and Power, or in order to forward the more dangerous Designs of a Faction, *to both which a*

*Peace would have put an End; And that the Part of the War which
was chiefly our Province, which would have been most beneficial to
us, and destructive to the Enemy, was wholly neglected. As to a Peace,
We complain of being deluded by a* Mock Treaty; *in which those
who Negotiated, took care to make such Demands as they knew were
impossible to be complied with, and therefore might securely press
every Article as if they were in earnest.*

*These are some of the Points I design to Treat of in the following
Discourse; with several others which I thought it necessary, at this
time, for the Kingdom to be informed of. I think I am not mistaken
in those Facts I mention; at least not in any Circumstance so material,
as to weaken the Consequences I draw from them.*

After Ten Years War, *with perpetual Success, to tell us it is yet
impossible to have a good Peace, is very surprising, and seems so
different from what hath ever hapned in the World before, that a Man
of any Party may be allowed suspecting, we have either been ill
used, or have not made the most of our Victories, and might therefore
desire to know where the Difficulty lay: Then it is natural to enquire
into our present Condition; how long we shall be able to go on at this
Rate; what the Consequences may be upon the present and future
Ages; and whether a Peace, without that impracticable Point which
some People do so much insist on, be really ruinous in it self, or equally
so with the Continuance of the War.*

THE

CONDUCT

OF THE

ALLIES, &c.

THE Motives that may engage a wise Prince or State in a War, I take to be one or more of these: Either to check the overgrown Power of some ambitious Neighbour; to recover what hath been unjustly taken from Them; to revenge some Injury They have received; (which all Political Casuists allow); to assist some Ally in a just Quarrel; or lastly, to defend Themselves when They are invaded. In all these Cases, the Writers upon Politicks admit a War to be justly undertaken. The last is what hath been usually called *pro aris & focis*; where no Expence or Endeavour can be too great, because all we have is at stake, and consequently, our utmost Force to be exerted; and the Dispute is soon determined, either in Safety or utter Destruction. But in the other four, I believe, it will be found, that no Monarch or Commonwealth did ever engage beyond a certain Degree; never proceeding so far as to exhaust the Strength and Substance of their Country by Anticipations and Loans, which, in a few Years, must put them in a worse Condition than any they could reasonably apprehend from those Evils, for the preventing of which they first entred into the War: Because this would be to run into real infallible Ruin, only in hopes to remove what might perhaps but appear so by a probable Speculation.

AND, as a War should be undertaken upon a just and prudent Motive, so it is still more obvious, that a Prince ought maturely to consider the Condition he is in, when he enters on it: Whether his Coffers be full, his Revenues clear of Debts, his People numerous and rich by a long Peace and free Trade, not overpressed with many burthensom Taxes; No violent

Faction ready to dispute his just Prerogative, and thereby weaken his Authority at Home, and lessen his Reputation Abroad. For, if the contrary of all this happen to be his Case, he will hardly be persuaded to disturb the World's Quiet and his own, while there is any other way left of preserving the latter with Honour and Safety.

SUPPOSING the War to have commenced upon a just Motive; the next Thing to be considered, is, When a Prince ought in Prudence to receive the Overtures of a Peace: Which I take to be, either when the Enemy is ready to yield the Point originally contended for, or when that Point is found impossible to be ever obtained; or when contending any longer, though with Probability of gaining that Point at last, would put such a Prince and his People in a worse Condition than the present Loss of it. All which Considerations are of much greater Force, where a War is managed by an Alliance of many Confederates, which in the variety of Interests, among the several Parties, is liable to so many unforeseen Accidents.

IN a Confederate War it ought to be considered, which Party has the deepest share in the Quarrel: For though each may have their particular Reasons, yet one or two among them will probably be more concerned than the rest, and therefore ought to bear the greatest part of the Burthen, in proportion to their Strength. For Example: Two Princes may be Competitors for a Kingdom, and it will be your Interest to take the Part of Him, who will probably allow you good Conditions of Trade, rather than of the other, who possibly may not. However, that Prince whose Cause you espouse, though never so vigorously, is the Principal in that War, and You, properly speaking, are but a Second. Or a Commonwealth may lie in danger to be over-run by a powerful Neighbour, which, in time, may produce very bad Consequences upon your Trade and Liberty: 'Tis therefore necessary, as well as prudent, to lend them Assistance, and help them to win a strong secure Frontier; but, as They must in course be the first and greatest Sufferers, so, in Justice, they ought to bear the greatest Weight. If a House be on fire, it behoves all in the Neighbourhood to run with Buckets to quench it; but the Owner is sure to be undone first; and it is not impossible that those at next Door may escape, by a Shower from Heaven, or the stillness of the Weather, or some other favourable Accident.

But, if an Ally, who is not so immediately concerned in the good or ill Fortune of the War, be so generous, as to contribute more than the Principal Party, and even more in proportion to his Abilities, he ought at least to have his Share in what is conquered from the Enemy: Or, if his Romantick Disposition transports him so far, as to expect little or nothing of this, he might however hope, that the Principals would make it up in Dignity and Respect; and he would surely think it monstrous to find them intermedling in his Domestick Affairs, prescribing what Servants he should keep or dismiss, pressing him perpetually with the most unreasonable Demands, and at every turn threatning to break the Alliance, if he will not comply.

From these Reflections upon War in general, I descend to consider those Wars, wherein *England* hath been engaged since the Conquest. In the Civil-Wars of the *Barons*, as well as those between the Houses of *York* and *Lancaster*, great Destruction was made of the Nobility and Gentry, new Families raised, and old ones extinguished, but the Money spent on both sides was employed and circulated at Home; no Publick Debts contracted; and a very few Years of Peace quickly set all right again.

The like may be affirmed even of that unnatural Rebellion against King *Charles* I. the Usurpers maintained great Armies in constant Pay, had almost continual War with *Spain* or *Holland*, but managing it by their Fleets, they encreased very much the Riches of the Kingdom, instead of exhausting them.

Our Foreign Wars were generally against *Scotland* or *France*; the first being upon our own Continent, carried no Money out of the Kingdom, and were seldom of long continuance. During our first Wars with *France*, we possessed great Dominions in that Country, where we preserved some Footing till the Reign of Queen *Mary*; and though some of our latter Princes made very chargeable Expeditions thither, a Subsidy, and two or three Fifteenths, cleared all the Debt. Beside, our Victories were then of some Use as well as Glory; for we were so prudent to Fight, and so happy to Conquer, only for our selves.

THE *Dutch* Wars, in the Reign of King *Charles* II. though begun and carried on under a very corrupt Administration, and much to the Dishonour of the Crown, did indeed keep the King needy and poor, by discontinuing or discontenting his Parliament, when he most needed their Assistance; but neither left any Debt upon the Nation, nor carried any Mony out of it.

AT the *Revolution*, a general War broke out in *Europe*, wherein many Princes joined in an Alliance against *France*, to check the ambitious Designs of that Monarch; and here the *Emperor*, the *Dutch*, and *England* were Principals. About this time the Custom first began among us of borrowing Millions upon Funds of Interest: It was pretended, That the War could not possibly last above one or two Campaigns; and that the Debts contracted might be easily paid in a few Years, by a gentle Tax, without burthening the Subject. But the true Reason for embracing this Expedient, was the Security of a new Prince, not firmly settled on the Throne: People were tempted to lend, by great Premiums and large Interest, and it concerned them nearly to preserve that Government, which they trusted with their Money. The Person said to have been Author of so detestable a Project, is still living, and lives to see some of its fatal Consequences, whereof his Grand-Children will not see an end. And this pernicious Counsel closed very well with the Posture of Affairs at that time: For, a Set of Upstarts, who had little or no part in the *Revolution*, but valued themselves by their Noise and pretended Zeal when the Work was over, were got into Credit at Court, by the Merit of becoming Undertakers and Projectors of Loans and Funds: These, finding that the Gentlemen of Estates were not willing to come into their Measures, fell upon those new Schemes of raising Mony, in order to create a Mony'd-Interest, that might in time vie with the Landed, and of which they hoped to be at the Head.

THE Ground of the first War, for ten Years after the *Revolu-*

tion, as to the Part we had in it, was, to make *France* acknowledge the late King, and to recover *Hudson's-Bay*. But during that whole War, the Sea was almost entirely neglected, and the greatest Part of *Six* Millions Annually employed to enlarge the Frontier of the *Dutch*. For the King was a General, but not an Admiral; and although King of *England*, was a Native of *Holland*.

AFTER ten Years Fighting to little purpose; after the Loss of above an hundred thousand Men, and a Debt remaining of twenty Millions, we at length hearkned to the Terms of a Peace, which was concluded with great Advantages to the *Empire* and *Holland*, but none at all to us; and clogged soon after by the famous Treaty of *Partition*; by which, *Naples*, *Sicily*, and *Lorain*, were to be added to the *French* Dominions; or if that Crown should think fit to set aside the Treaty, upon the *Spaniards* refusing to accept it, as they declared they would, to the several Parties at the very time of transacting it; then the *French* would have Pretensions to the whole Monarchy. And so it proved in the Event; for, the late King of *Spain* reckoning it an Indignity to have his Territories cantoned out into Parcels, by other Princes, during his own Life, and without his Consent, rather chose to bequeath the Monarchy entire to a younger Son of *France*: And this Prince was acknowledged for King of *Spain* both by Us and *Holland*.

IT must be granted, that the Counsels of entring into the present War were violently opposed by the *Church-Party*, who first advised the late King to acknowledge the Duke of *Anjou*; and particularly, 'tis affirmed that the Earl of *Godolphin*, who was then in the Church-Interest, told the King in *November*, 1701, That since his Majesty was determined to engage in a War so contrary to his private Opinion, he could serve him no longer, and accordingly gave up his Employment; though he happened afterwards to change his Mind, when he was to be Lord High Treasurer, and have the sole Management of Affairs at home; while those abroad were to be in the hands of *One*, whose Advantage, by all sorts of Ties, he was engaged to promote.

THE Declarations of War against *France* and *Spain*, made by

Us and *Holland,* are dated within a few Days of each other. In that published by the *States,* they say very truly, That *they are nearest, and most exposed to the Fire;* that *they are blocked up on all sides, and actually attacked by the Kings of* France *and* Spain; that *their Declaration is the Effect of an urgent and pressing Necessity;* with other Expressions to the same purpose. They *desire the Assistance of all Kings and Princes,* &c. The grounds of their Quarrel with *France,* are such as only affect themselves, or at least more immediately than any other Prince or State; such as, *the* French *refusing to grant the Tariff promised by the Treaty of* Ryswick; *the loading the* Dutch *Inhabitants settled in* France, *with excessive Duties, contrary to the said Treaty; the Violation of the* Partition-Treaty, *by the* French *accepting the King of* Spain's *Will, and threatning the* States, *if they would not comply; the seizing the* Spanish Netherlands *by the* French *Troops, and turning out the* Dutch, *who by Permission of the late King of* Spain *were in Garrison there; by which means that Republick was deprived of her Barrier, contrary to the Treaty of* Partition, *where it was particularly stipulated, that the* Spanish Netherlands *should be left to the Archduke.* They alledged, that *the* French *King governed* Flanders *as his own, though under the Name of his Grandson, and sent great Numbers of Troops thither to fright them: That he had seized the City and Citadel of* Liege, *had possessed himself of several Places in the Archbishoprick of* Cologne, *and maintained Troops in the Country of* Wolfenbuttel, *in order to block up the* Dutch *on all sides; and caused his Resident to give in a Memorial, wherein he threatned the* States *to act against them, if they refused complying with the Contents of that Memorial.*

THE Queen's Declaration of War is grounded upon the *Grand Alliance,* as This was upon the unjust Usurpations and Encroachments of the *French* King; whereof the Instances produced are, *His keeping in Possession a great Part of the* Spanish *Dominions, seizing* Milan *and the* Spanish *Low-Countries, making himself Master of* Cadiz, *&c. And instead of giving Satisfaction in these Points, his putting an Indignity and Affront on Her Majesty and Kingdoms, by Declaring the Pretended Prince of* Wales *King of* England, *&c.* which last was the only personal Quarrel we had in the War; and even This was positively denied by

France, That King being then willing to Acknowledge Her Majesty.

I THINK it plainly appears, by both Declarations, that *England* ought no more to have been a Principal in this War, than *Prussia*, or any other Power, who came afterwards into that Alliance. *Holland* was first in the Danger, the *French* Troops being at that time just at the Gates of *Nimeguen*. But the Complaints made in our Declaration, do all, except the last, as much or more concern almost every Prince in *Europe*.

FOR, among the several Parties who came first or last into this Confederacy, there were few but who, in proportion, had more to get or to lose, to hope or to fear, from the good or ill Success of this War, than We. The *Dutch* took up Arms to defend themselves from immediate Ruin; and by a successful War, they proposed to have a larger Extent of Country, and a better Frontier against *France*. The *Emperor* hoped to recover the Monarchy of *Spain*, or some part of it, for his younger Son, chiefly at the Expence of Us and *Holland*. The King of *Portugal* had received Intelligence, that *Philip* designed to renew the old Pretensions of *Spain* upon that Kingdom, which is surrounded by the other on all sides, except towards the Sea, and could therefore only be defended by *Maritime Powers*. This, with the advantageous Terms offered by King *Charles*, as well as by Us, prevailed with that Prince to enter into the Alliance. The Duke of *Savoy*'s Temptations and Fears were yet greater: The main Charge of the War on that side, was to be supplied by *England*, and the Profit to redound to him. In case *Milan* should be Conquered, it was stipulated that his Royal Highness should have the Dutchy of *Montferrat*, belonging to the Duke of *Mantua*, the Provinces of *Alexandria*, and *Valentia*, and *Lomellino*, with other Lands between the *Po* and the *Tanaro*, together with the *Vigevenasco*, or in lieu of it, an Equivalent out of the Province of *Novara*, adjoining to his own State; beside whatever else could be taken from *France* on that side by the Confederate Forces. Then, he was in terrible Apprehensions of being surrounded by *France*, who had so many Troops in the *Milanese*, and might have easily swallowed up his whole Dutchy.

THE rest of the Allies came in purely for Subsidies, whereof they sunk considerable Sums into their own Coffers, and refused to send their *Contingent* to the *Emperor*, alledging their Troops were already hired by *England* and *Holland*.

SOME time after the Duke of *Anjou*'s succeeding to the Monarchy of *Spain*, in breach of the *Partition* Treaty, the Question here in *England* was, Whether the Peace should be continued, or a new War begun. Those who were for the former, alledged the Debts and Difficulties we laboured under; that both We and the *Dutch* had already Acknowledged *Philip* for King of *Spain*; that the Inclinations of the *Spaniards* to the House of *Austria*, and their Aversion for that of *Bourbon*, were not so surely to be reckoned upon, as some would pretend; that We rightly thought it a piece of Insolence, as well as Injustice, in the *French*, to offer putting a King upon Us; and the *Spaniards* would conceive, we had as little Reason to force one upon Them; That it was true, the Nature and Genius of those two People differed very much, and so would probably continue to do, as well under a King of *French* Blood, as one of *Austrian*; but, if we should engage in a War for Dethroning the Duke of *Anjou*, we should certainly effect what, by the Progress and Operations of it, we endeavoured to prevent, I mean an Union of Interest and Affections between the two Nations; For the *Spaniards* must of necessity call in *French* Troops to their Assistance: This would introduce *French* Counsellors into King *Philip*'s Court; and this, by degrees, would habituate and reconcile the two Nations: That, to assist King *Charles* by *English* or *Dutch* Forces, would render him odious to his new Subjects, who have nothing in so great an Abomination, as those whom they hold for *Hereticks:* That, the *French* would by this means become Masters of the Treasures in the *Spanish West-Indies:* That, in the last War, when *Spain*, *Cologne*, and *Bavaria* were in our Alliance, and by a modest Computation brought Sixty thousand Men into the Field against the Common Enemy; when *Flanders*, the Seat of War, was on our side, and his Majesty, a Prince of great Valour and Conduct, at the Head of the whole Confederate Army; yet we had no Reason to boast of our Success: How then should we be able to oppose *France* with those Powers against us, which would carry Sixty thousand Men from us to the Enemy, and so make us, upon the Balance, weaker by One hundred and twenty thousand Men, at the beginning of this War, than of that in the Year 1688?

ON the other side, those whose Opinion, or some private Motives, inclined them to give their Advice for entring into a new War, alledged how dangerous it would be for *England*, that *Philip* should be King of *Spain*; that we could have no Security for our Trade, while that Kingdom was subject to a Prince of the *Bourbon* Family; nor any hopes of preserving the Balance of *Europe*, because the Grandfather would, in effect, be King, while his Grandson had but the Title, and thereby have a better Opportunity than ever of pursuing his Design for Universal Monarchy. These and the like Arguments prevailed; and so, without offering at any other Remedy, without taking time to consider the Consequences, or to reflect on our own Condition, we hastily engaged in a War which hath cost us sixty Millions; and after repeated, as well as unexpected Success in Arms, hath put us and our Posterity in a worse Condition, not only than any of our Allies, but even our conquered Enemies themselves.

THE part we have acted in the Conduct of this whole War, with reference to our Allies abroad, and to a prevailing Faction at home, is what I shall now particularly examin; where I presume it will appear, by plain Matters of Fact, that no Nation was ever so long or so scandalously abused by the Folly, the Temerity, the Corruption, the Ambition of its domestick Enemies; or treated with so much Insolence, Injustice and Ingratitude by its foreign Friends.

THIS will be manifest by proving the Three following Points.

First, That against all manner of Prudence or common Reason, we engaged in this War as Principals, when we ought to have acted only as Auxiliaries.

Secondly, That we spent all our Vigour in pursuing that Part of the War which could least answer the End we proposed by beginning of it; and made no Efforts at all where we could have most weakned the Common Enemy, and at the same time enriched our Selves.

Lastly, That we suffered each of our Allies to break every Article in those Treaties and Agreements by which they were bound, and to lay the Burthen upon us.

UPON the first of these Points, That we ought to have entered into this War only as Auxiliaries. Let any Man reflect upon our Condition at that time: Just come out of the most tedious, expensive and unsuccessful War that ever *England* had been engaged in; sinking under heavy Debts, of a Nature and Degree never heard of by Us or Our Ancestors; the Bulk of the Gentry and People heartily tired of the War, and glad of a Peace, though it brought no other Advantage but it self: No sudden Prospect of lessening our Taxes, which were grown as necessary to pay our Debts, as to raise Armies: A sort of artificial Wealth of Funds and Stocks in the Hands of those who for Ten Years before had been plundering the Publick; Many Corruptions in every Branch of our Government, that needed Reformation. Under these Difficulties, from which Twenty Years Peace, and the wisest Management, could hardly recover us, we declare War against *France*, fortified by the Accession and Alliance of those Powers I mentioned before, and which, in the former War, had been Parties in our Confederacy. It is very obvious what a Change must be made in the Balance, by such Weights taken out of Our Scale and put into Theirs; since it was manifest by Ten Years Experience, that *France* without those Additions of Strength, was able to maintain it self against us. So that Human Probability ran with mighty odds on the other side; and in that case, nothing under the most extreme Necessity should force any State to engage in a War. We had already acknowledged *Philip* for King of *Spain*; neither does the Queen's Declaration of War take notice of the Duke of *Anjou*'s Succession to that Monarchy, as a Subject of Quarrel; but the *French* King's governing it as if it were his own; his seizing *Cadiz*, *Milan*, and the *Spanish Low Countries*, with the Indignity of Proclaiming the *Pretender*. In all which we charge that Prince with nothing directly relating to us, excepting the last: And this, although indeed a great Affront, might have easily been redressed without a War; for the *French* Court declared they did not acknowledge the *Pretender*, but only gave him the Title of *King*, which was allowed to *Augustus* by his Enemy of *Sueden*, who had driven him out of *Poland*, and forced him to acknowledge *Stanislaus*.

'T is true indeed, the Danger of the *Dutch*, by so ill a Neighbourhood in *Flanders*, might affect us very much in the Consequences of it; and the Loss of *Spain* to the House of *Austria*, if it should be governed by *French* Influence, and *French* Politicks, might, in time, be very pernicious to our Trade. It would therefore have been prudent, as well as generous and charitable, to help our Neighbour; and so we might have done without injuring our selves: For by an old Treaty with *Holland*, we were bound to assist that Republick with Ten thousand Men, whenever they were attacked by the *French*; whose Troops, upon the King of *Spain*'s Death, taking Possession of *Flanders*, in right of *Philip*, and securing the *Dutch* Garrisons 'till they would acknowledge Him, the *States-General*, by Memorials from their Envoy here, demanded only the Ten thousand Men, we were obliged to give them by virtue of that Treaty. And I make no doubt but *Holland* would have exerted themselves so vigorously, as to be able, with that Assistance alone, to defend their Frontiers: Or, if they had been forced to a Peace, the *Spaniards*, who abhor dismembring their Monarchy, would never have suffered the *French* to possess themselves of *Flanders*. At that time they had none of those Endearments to each other which this War hath created; and whatever Hatred and Jealousie were natural between the two Nations, would then have appeared. So that there was no sort of necessity for Us to proceed further, although We had been in a better Condition. But our Politicians at that time had other Views, and a new War must be undertaken, upon the Advice of those, who with their Partisans and Adherents, were to be the sole Gainers by it. A Grand Alliance was therefore made between the Emperor, *England*, and the *States-General*; by which, if the Injuries complained of from *France* were not remedied in two Months, the Parties concerned were obliged mutually to assist each other *with their whole Strength*.

THUS We became Principal in a War, in Conjunction with two Allies, whose share in the Quarrel was, beyond all Proportion, greater than Ours. However, I can see no Reason from the Words of the Grand Alliance, by which we were obliged to make those prodigious Expences we have since been at. By what I have always heard and read, I take the *whole Strength of the Nation*, as understood in that Treaty, to be the utmost that a Prince can raise Annually from his Subjects; if he be forced to Mortgage and Borrow, whether at Home or Abroad, it is not, properly speaking, *his own Strength*, or that of the Nation, but the entire Substance of particular Persons, which not being able to raise out of the annual Income of his Kingdom, he takes upon Security, and can only pay the Interest; and by this Method one Part of the Nation is pawned to the other, with hardly a Possibility left of being ever redeemed.

SURELY it would have been enough for us to have suspended the Payment of our Debts contracted in the former War, to have continued our Land and Malt Tax, with those others which have since been mortgaged: These, with some Additions, would have made up such a Sum, as, with prudent Management, might, I suppose, have maintained an Hundred thousand Men by Sea and Land; a reasonable Quota in all conscience for that Ally, who apprehended least Danger, and expected least Advantage. Nor can we imagine that either of the Confederates, when the War begun, would have been so unreasonable, as to refuse joyning with us upon such a Foot, and expect that we should every Year go between three and four Millions in Debt (which hath been our Case) because the *French* could hardly have contrived any Offers of a Peace so ruinous to us as such a War. Posterity will be at a loss to conceive what kind of Spirit could possess their Ancestors, who after ten Years Suffering, by the unexampled Politicks of a Nation, maintaining a War by annually Pawning it self; and during a short Peace, while they were looking back with Horrour on the heavy Load of Debts they had contracted; universally condemning those pernicious Counsels which had occasioned them; racking their Invention for some Remedies or Expedients to mend their shattered Condition: That these very People, without giving themselves time to breath, should again enter into a more dangerous, chargeable, and extensive War, for the same, or perhaps a greater Period of Time, and without any apparent Necessity. It is obvious in a private Fortune, that whoever annually runs out, and continues the same Expences, must every Year mortgage a greater Quantity of Land than he did before; and as the Debt doubles and trebles upon him, so doth his Inability to pay it. By the same Proportion we have suffered twice as much by this last ten Years War, as we did by the former; and if it were possible to continue it five Years longer at the same rate, it would be as great a Burthen as the whole Twenty. This Computation, so easy and trivial as it is almost a shame to mention, Posterity will think that those who first advised the War, had either not the Sense or the Honesty to consider.

AND as we have wasted our Strength and vital Substance in this profuse manner, so we have shamefully misapplied it to Ends at least very different from those for which we undertook the War, and often to effect others which after a Peace we may severely repent. This is the second Article I proposed to examine.

WE have now for Ten Years together turned the whole Force and Expence of the War, where the Enemy was best able to hold us at a Bay; where we could propose no manner of Advantage to our selves; where it was highly impolitick to enlarge our Conquests; utterly neglecting that Part which would have saved and gained us many Millions, which the perpetual Maxims of our Government teach us to pursue; which would have soonest weakened the Enemy, and must either have promoted a speedy Peace, or enabled us to go on with the War.

THOSE who are fond of continuing the War cry up our constant Success at a most prodigious rate, and reckon it infinitely greater than in all human Probability we had reason to hope. Ten glorious Compaigns are passed, and now at last, like the sick Man, we are just expiring with all sorts of good Symptoms. Did the Advisers of this War suppose it would continue Ten Years, without expecting the Successes we have had; and yet at the same time determine, that *France* must be reduced, and *Spain* subdued, by employing our whole Strength upon *Flanders?* Did they believe the last War left us in a Condition to furnish such vast Supplies for so long a Period, without involving Us and our Posterity in unextricable Debts? If after such Miraculous *Doings*, we are not yet in a Condition of bringing *France* to our Terms, nor can tell when we shall be so, though we should proceed without any Reverse of Fortune; What could we look for in the ordinary course of Things, but a *Flanders* War of at least Twenty Years longer? Do they indeed think a Town taken for the *Dutch*, is a sufficient Recompence to us for six Millions of Money? which is of so little Consequence to the determining the War, that the *French* may yet hold out a dozen Years more, and afford a Town every Campaign at the same Price.

I say not this, by any means, to detract from the Army or its Leaders. Getting into the Enemy's Lines, passing Rivers, and taking Towns, may be Actions attended with many glorious Circumstances: But when all this brings no real solid Advantage to us, when it hath no other End than to enlarge the Territories of the *Dutch*, and encrease the Fame and Wealth of our *General*, I conclude, however it comes about, that Things are not as they should be; and that surely our Forces and Money might be better employed, both towards reducing our Enemy, and working out some Benefit to our selves. But the Case is still much harder, We are destroying many thousand Lives, exhausting all our Substance, not for our own Interest, which would be but common Prudence; not for a Thing indifferent, which would be sufficient Folly, but perhaps to our own Destruction, which is perfect Madness. We may live to feel the Effects of our Valour more sensibly than all the Consequences we imagine from the Dominions of *Spain* in the Duke of *Anjou.* We have Conquered a noble

Territory for the *States*, that will maintain sufficient Troops to Defend it self, feed many hundred thousand Inhabitants, where all Encouragement will be given to introduce and improve Manufactures, which was the only Advantage they wanted; and which, added to their Skill, Industry and Parsimony, will enable them to undersell us in every Market of the World.

OUR Supply of Forty thousand Men, according to the first Stipulation, added to the Quota's of the Emperor and *Holland*, which they were obliged to furnish, would have made an Army of near Two hundred thousand, exclusive of Garrisons; enough to withstand all the Power that *France* could bring against it; and we might have employed the rest much better, both for the common Cause and our own Advantage.

THE War in *Spain* must be imputed to the Credulity of our Ministers, who suffered themselves to be persuaded by the Imperial Court, that the *Spaniards* were so violently affected to the House of *Austria*, as upon the first Appearance there, with a few Troops under the Archduke, the whole Kindom would immediately revolt. This we tried, and found the Emperor to have deceived either Us or Himself: Yet there we drove on the War at a prodigious Disadvantage, with great Expence; And by a most corrupt Management, the only General, who by a Course of Conduct and Fortune almost miraculous, had nearly put us into Possession of the Kingdom, was left wholly unsupported, exposed to the Envy of his Rivals, disappointed by the Caprices of a young unexperienced Prince, under the Guidance of a rapacious *German* Ministry, and at last called home in Discontent: By which our Armies, both in *Spain* and *Portugal*, were made a Sacrifice to Avarice, Ill-conduct, or Treachery.

IN common Prudence, we should either have pushed that War with the utmost Vigor, in so fortunate a Juncture, especially since the gaining that Kingdom was the great Point for which we pretended to continue the War, or at least when we had *found* or *made* that Design impracticable, we should not have gone on in so expensive a Management of it; but have kept our Troops on the Defensive in *Catalonia*, and pursued

D

some other way more effectual for distressing the Common Enemy, and advantaging Ourselves.

AND what a noble Field of Honour and Profit had we before us, wherein to employ the best of our Strength, which, against all the Maxims of *British* Policy, we suffered to lie wholly neglected? I have sometimes wondered how it came to pass, that the Style of *Maritime Powers*, by which our Allies, in a sort of contemptuous manner, usually couple us with the *Dutch*, did never put us in mind of the Sea; and while some Politicians were shewing us the way to *Spain* by *Flanders*, others by *Savoy* or *Naples*, that the *West-Indies* should never come into their Heads. With half the Charge we have been at, we might have maintained our original Quota of Forty thousand Men in *Flanders*, and at the same time, by our Fleets and Naval Forces, have so distressed the *Spaniards* in the North and South Seas of *America*, as to prevent any Returns of Mony from thence, except in our own Bottoms. This is what best became us to do as a Maritime Power: This, with any common-degree of Success, would soon have compelled *France* to the Necessities of a Peace, and *Spain* to acknowledge the Archduke. But while We, for Ten Years, have been squandring away our Mony upon the Continent, *France* hath been wisely engrossing all the Trade of *Peru*, going directly with their Ships to *Lima*, and other Ports, and there receiving Ingots of Gold and Silver for *French* Goods of little Value; which, beside the mighty Advantage to their Nation at present, may divert the Channel of that Trade for the future, so beneficial to us, who used to receive annually such vast Sums at *Cadiz*, for our Goods sent thence to the *Spanish West-Indies*. All this we tamely saw and suffered, without the least Attempt to hinder it; except what was performed by some private Men at *Bristol*, who inflamed by a true Spirit of Courage and Industry, did, about three Years ago, with a few Vessels, fitted out at their own Charge, make a most successful Voyage into those Parts, took one of the *Aquapulco* Ships, very narrowly mist of the other, and are lately returned laden with unenvied Wealth; to shew us what might have been done with the like Management, by a publick Undertaking. At least we might easily have prevented those great Returns of Mony to *France* and *Spain*, though we could not have taken it our selves. And if it be true, as the Advocates for War would have it, that the *French* are now so impoverished; in what Condition must they have been, if that Issue of Wealth had been stopped?

BUT great Events often turn upon very small Circumstances. It was the Kingdom's Misfortune, that the Sea was not the Duke of *Marlborough*'s Element, otherwise the whole Force of the War would infallibly have been bestowed there, infinitely to the Advantage of his Country, which would then have gone hand in hand with his own. But it is very truly objected, That if we alone had made such an Attempt as this, *Holland* would have been Jealous; or if we had done it in Conjunction with *Holland*, the House of *Austria* would have been discontented. This hath been the Style of late Years; which whoever introduced among us, they have taught our Allies to speak after them. Otherwise it could hardly enter into any Imagination, that while we are Confederates in a War, with those who are to have the whole Profit, and who leave a double share of the Burthen upon Us, we dare not think of any Design, though against the Common Enemy, where there is the least Prospect of doing Good to our own Country, for fear of giving Umbrage and Offence to our Allies; while we are ruining our selves to Conquer Provinces and Kingdoms for Them. I therefore confess with Shame, that this Objection is true: For it is very well known, that while the Design of Mr. *Hill*'s Expedition remained a Secret, it was suspected in *Holland* and *Germany* to be intended against *Peru*; whereupon the *Dutch* made every where their Publick Complaints, and the Ministers at *Vienna* talked of it as *an Insolence in the Queen to attempt such an Undertaking*; which, however it has failed, partly by the Accidents of a Storm, and partly by the Stubbornness or Treachery of some in that Colony, for whose Relief, and at whose Entreaty it was in some measure designed, is no Objection at all to an Enterprize so well concerted, and with such fair Probability of Success.

IT was something singular that the *States* should express their Uneasiness, when they thought we intended to make some

Attempt in the *Spanish West-Indies*; because it is agreed between us, that whatever is Conquered there, by Us or Them, shall belong to the Conqueror: Which is the only Article that I can call to mind, in all our Treaties or Stipulations, with any view of Interest to this Kingdom; and for that very Reason, I suppose, among others, hath been altogether neglected. Let those who think this too severe a Reflection, examin the whole Management of the present War by Sea and Land with all our Alliances, Treaties, Stipulations and Conventions, and consider, whether the whole does not look as if some particular Care and Industry had been used, to prevent any Benefit or Advantage that might possibly accrue to *Britain*.

THIS kind of Treatment from our two Principal Allies, hath taught the same Dialect to all the rest; so that there is hardly a petty Prince, whom we half maintain by Subsidies and Pensions, who is not ready, upon every Occasion, to threaten Us, that He will recal His Troops (though they must rob or starve at home) if we refuse to comply with Him in any Demand, however so unreasonable.

UPON the Third Head I shall produce some Instances, to shew how tamely we have suffered each of our Allies to infringe every Article in those Treaties and Stipulations by which they were bound, and to lay the Load upon Us.

BUT before I enter upon this, which is a large Subject, I shall take leave to offer a few Remarks on certain Articles in three of our Treaties; which may let us perceive, how much those Ministers valued or understood the true Interest, Safety, or Honour of their Country.

WE have made two Alliances with *Portugal*, an Offensive and Defensive: The first is to remain in force only during the present War; the second to be Perpetual. In the Offensive Alliance, the Emperor, *England*, and *Holland* are Parties with *Portugal*; in the Defensive only We and the *States*.

UPON the first Article of the Offensive Alliance it is to be observed, that although the Grand Alliance, as I have already said, allows *England* and *Holland* to possess for their own, whatever each of them shall Conquer in the *Spanish West-*

Indies; yet here we are quite cut out, by consenting, that the Arch-Duke shall possess the Dominions of *Spain* in as full a manner as their late King *Charles*. And what is more remarkable, we broke this very Article in favour of *Portugal*, by subsequent Stipulations; where we agree, that King *Charles* shall deliver up *Estremadura*, *Vigo*, and some other Places to the *Portuguese*, as soon as we can Conquer them from the Enemy. They who were guilty of so much Folly and Contradiction, know best whether it proceeded from Corruption or Stupidity.

BY two other Articles (beside the Honour of being Convoys and Guards in ordinary to the *Portuguese* Ships and Coasts) we are to guess the Enemies Thoughts, and to take the King of *Portugal*'s Word, whenever he has a Fancy that he shall be invaded: We also are to furnish him with a Strength superior to what the Enemy intends to invade any of his Dominions with, let that be what it will: And, 'till we know what the Enemy's Forces are, His *Portuguese* Majesty is sole Judge what Strength is superior, and what will be able to prevent an Invasion; and may send our Fleets, whenever he pleases, upon his Errands, to some of the furthest Parts of the World, or keep them attending upon his own Coasts till he thinks fit to dismiss them. These Fleets must likewise be subject, in all things, not only to the King, but to his Viceroys, Admirals and Governours, in any of his foreign Dominions, when he is in a Humour to apprehend an Invasion; which, I believe, is an Indignity that was never offered before, except to a Conquered Nation.

IN the Defensive Alliance with that Crown, which is to remain perpetual, and where only *England* and *Holland* are Parties with them, the same Care, in almost the same Words, is taken for our Fleet to attend their Coasts and foreign Dominions, and to be under the same Obedience. We and the *States* are likewise to furnish them with twelve Thousand Men at our own Charge, which we are constantly to recruit, and these are to be subject to the *Portuguese* Generals.

IN the Offensive Alliance we took no care of having the Assistance of *Portugal*, whenever we should be invaded: But in this, it seems, we were wiser; for that King is obliged to make War on *France* or *Spain*, whenever we or *Holland* are invaded by either; but before this, we are to supply them with the same Forces, both by Sea and Land, as if he were invaded himself: And this must needs be a very prudent and safe Course for a Maritime Power to take upon a sudden Invasion; by which, instead of making use of our Fleets and Armies for our own Defence, we must send them abroad for the Defence of *Portugal*.

By the Thirteenth Article we are told, what this Assistance is which the *Portugueze* are to give us, and upon what Conditions. They are to furnish Ten Men of War; and when *England* or *Holland* shall be invaded by *France* and *Spain* together, or by *Spain* alone; in either of these Cases, those Ten *Portugueze* Men of War are to serve only upon their own Coasts; where, no doubt, they will be of mighty Use to their Allies, and Terror to the Enemy.

How the *Dutch* were drawn to have a Part in either of these two Alliances, is not very material to enquire, since they have been so wise as never to observe them, nor, I suppose, ever intended it, but resolved, as they have since done, to shift the Load upon us.

Let any Man read these two Treaties from the beginning to the end, he will imagine, that the King of *Portugal* and his Ministers sat down and made them by themselves, and then sent them to their Allies to Sign; the whole Spirit and Tenor of them, quite thro', running only upon this single Point, What We and *Holland* are to do for *Portugal*, without any mention of an Equivalent, except those Ten Ships, which at the time when we have greatest need of their Assistance, are obliged to attend upon their own Coasts.

The Barrier-Treaty between *Great Britain* and *Holland*, was concluded at the *Hague* on the 29th of *October*, in the Year 1709. In this Treaty, neither Her Majesty, nor Her Kingdoms, have any Interest or Concern, farther than what is mentioned in the Second and the Twentieth Articles: By the former, the States are to assist the Queen in Defending the Act of Succession; and by the other, not to Treat of a Peace 'till *France* acknowledges the Queen and the Succession of *Hanover*, and promises to remove the *Pretender* out of his Dominions.

As to the first of these, It is certainly for the Safety and Interest of the *States-General*, that the Protestant Succession should be preserved in *England*; because such a Popish Prince as we apprehend, would infallibly join with *France* in the Ruin of that Republick. And the *Dutch* are as much bound to support our Succession, as they are tied to any Part of a Treaty or League Offensive and Defensive, against a Common Enemy, without any separate Benefit upon that Consideration. Her Majesty is in the full peaceable Possession of Her Kingdoms, and of the Hearts of Her People; among whom, hardly one in five hundred are in the *Pretender*'s Interest. And whether the Assistance of the *Dutch*, to preserve a Right so well established, be an Equivalent to those many unreasonable exorbitant Articles in the rest of the Treaty, let the World judge. What an Impression of our Settlement must it give Abroad, to see our Ministers offering such Conditions to the *Dutch*, to prevail on them to be Guarantees of our Acts of Parliament! Neither perhaps is it right, in point of Policy or good Sense, that a Foreign Power should be called in to confirm our Succession by way of Guarantee; but only to acknowledge it. Otherwise we put it out of the Power of our own Legislature to change our Succession, without the Consent of that Prince or State who is Guarantee; however our Posterity may hereafter, by the Tyranny and Oppression of any succeeding Princes, be reduced to the fatal Necessity of breaking in upon the excellent and happy Settlement now in force.

As to the other Article, it is a natural Consequence that must attend any Treaty of Peace we can make with *France*; being only the Acknowledgment of Her Majesty as Queen of Her own Dominions, and the Right of Succession by our own Laws, which no Foreign Power hath any Pretence to dispute.

However, in order to deserve these mighty Advantages from the *States*, the rest of the Treaty is wholly taken up in directing what we are to do for them.

By the Grand Alliance, which was the Foundation of the present War, the *Spanish Low-Countries* were to be recovered and delivered to the King of *Spain:* But by this Treaty, that Prince is to possess nothing in *Flanders* during the War: And after a Peace, the *States* are to have the Military Command of about twenty Towns with their Dependances, and four hundred thousand Crowns a Year from the King of *Spain* to maintain their Garrisons. By which means they will have the Command of all *Flanders*, from *Newport* on the Sea to *Namur* on the *Maese*, and be entirely Masters of the *Pais de Waas*, the richest part of those Provinces. Further, they have liberty to Garrison any Place they shall think fit in the *Spanish Low-Countries*, whenever there is an Appearance of War; and consequently to put Garrisons into *Ostend*, or where else they please, upon a Rupture with *England*.

By this Treaty likewise, the *Dutch* will, in effect, be entire Masters of all the *Low-Countries*, may impose Duties, Restrictions in Commerce, and Prohibitions at their Pleasure; and in that fertile Country may set up all sorts of Manufactures, particularly the Woollen, by inviting the disobliged Manufacturers in *Ireland*, and the *French* Refugees, who are scattered all over *Germany*. And as this Manufacture encreases abroad, the Cloathing People of *England* will be necessitated, for want of Employment, to follow; and in few Years, by help of the low Interest of Mony in *Holland*, *Flanders* may recover that beneficial Tráde which we got from them: The Landed Men of *England* will then be forced to re-establish the Staples of Wool abroad; and the *Dutch*, instead of being only the Carriers, will become the original Possessors of those Commodities, with which the greatest Part of the Trade of the World is now carried on. And as they increase their Trade, it is obvious they will enlarge their Strength at Sea, and that ours must lessen in Proportion.

All the Ports in *Flanders* are to be subject to the like Duties the *Dutch* shall lay upon the *Scheld*, which is to be closed on the side of the *States:* Thus all other Nations are, in effect, shut out from Trading with *Flanders*. Yet in the very same Article it is said, That the *States* shall be *favoured in all the Spanish Dominions as much as Great Britain, or as the People most favoured*. We have Conquered *Flanders* for them, and are in a worse

Condition, as to our Trade there, than before the War began. We have been the great Support of the King of *Spain*, to whom the *Dutch* have hardly contributed any thing at all; and yet *they are to be equally favoured with us in all his Dominions.* Of all this the Queen is under the unreasonable Obligation of being Guarantee, and that they shall possess their Barrier, and their four hundred thousand Crowns a Year, even before a Peace.

IT is to be observed, That this Treaty was only Signed by one of our Plenipotentiaries: And I have been told, That the other was heard to say, He would rather lose his Right-hand, than set it to such a Treaty. Had he spoke those Words in due season, and loud enough to be heard on this side the Water, considering the Credit he then had at Court, he might have saved much of his Country's Honour, and got as much to himself: Therefore, if the Report be true, I am inclined to think He only SAID it. I have been likewise told, That some very necessary Circumstances were wanting in the Entrance upon this Treaty; but the Ministers here rather chose to sacrifice the Honour of the Crown, and the Safety of their Country, than not ratify what one of their Favourites had transacted.

LET me now consider in what manner our Allies have observed those Treaties they made with Us, and the several Stipulations and Agreements pursuant to them.

BY the Grand Alliance between the Empire, *England* and *Holland*, we were to assist the other two, *totis viribus,* by Sea and Land. By a Convention subsequent to this Treaty, the Proportions which the several Parties should contribute towards the War, were adjusted in the following manner. The Emperor was obliged to furnish ninety Thousand Men against *France*, either in *Italy*, or upon the *Rhine: Holland* to bring sixty Thousand into the Field in *Flanders*, exclusive of Garrisons; and we forty Thousand. In Winter, 1702. which was the next Year, the Duke of *Marlborough* proposed the raising of Ten Thousand Men more, by way of Augmentation, and to carry on the War with greater Vigour; to which the Parliament agreed, and the *Dutch* were to raise the same Number. This was upon a *Par*, directly contrary to the former

Stipulation, whereby our Part was to be a Third less than theirs; and therefore it was granted, with a Condition, that *Holland* should break off all Trade and Commerce with *France*. But this Condition was never executed, the *Dutch* only amusing us with a specious Declaration till our Session of Parliament was ended; and the following Year it was taken off, by concert between our General and the *States*, without any Reason assigned for the Satisfaction of the Kingdom. The next and some ensuing Campaigns, further additional Forces were allowed by Parliament for the War in *Flanders*; and in every new Supply, the *Dutch* gradually lessened their Proportions; though the Parliament addressed the Queen that the *States* might be desired to observe them according to Agreement; which had no other Effect, than to teach them to elude it, by making their Troops Nominal Corps, as they did by keeping up the Numbers of Regiments, but sinking a fifth Part of the Men and Mony. So that now things are just inverted, and in all new Levies we contribute a third more than the *Dutch*, who at first were obliged to the same Proportion more than us.

BESIDES, the more Towns we Conquer for the *States*, the worse Condition we are in towards reducing the Common Enemy, and consequently of putting an end to the War. For they make no Scruple of employing the Troops of their Quota, towards Garrisoning every Town as fast as it is taken, directly contrary to the Agreement between us, by which all Garrisons are particularly excluded. This is at length arrived, by several Steps, to such a Height, that there are at present in the Field, not so many Forces under the Duke of *Marlborough*'s Command in *Flanders*, as *Britain* alone maintains for that Service, nor have been for some Years past. The Troops we maintain in *Flanders*, (as appears by the Votes of the House of Commons for the Year, 1709.) are Forty thousand the original Quota; Ten thousand the first Augmentation; three thousand *Palatines*; four thousand six hundred thirty nine *Saxons*; *Bothmer*'s Regiment of eight hundred Men; and a further Augmentation taken that Year into the Service of about two thousand; making in the whole upwards of sixty thousand:

THE CONDUCT of the ALLIES 31

And it is well known, that the Battles of *Hochstet* and *Ramellies* were fought with not above Fifty thousand Men on a side.

THE Duke of *Marlborough* having entered the Enemies Lines, and taking *Bouchain*, formed the Design of keeping so great a Number of Troops, and particularly of Cavalry, in *Lisle*, *Tournay*, *Doway*, and the Country between, as should be able to harass all the Neighbouring Provinces of *France*, during the Winter, prevent the Enemy from erecting their Magazines, and by consequence, from Subsisting their Forces next Spring, and render it impossible for them to assemble their Army another Year, without going back behind the *Soame* to do it. In order to effect this Project, it was necessary to be at an Expence extraordinary of Forage for the Troops, of building Stables, finding Fire and Candle for the Soldiers, with other incident Charges. The Queen readily agreed to furnish Her Share of the first Article, that of the Forage, which only belonged to Her. But the *States* insisting, that Her Majesty should likewise come into a Proportion of the other Articles, which in Justice belonged totally to them: She agreed even to that, rather than a Design of this Importance should fail. And yet we know it hath failed, and that the *Dutch* refused their Consent, 'till the time was past for putting it in Execution, even in the Opinion of those who proposed it. Perhaps a certain Article in the Treaties of Contributions, submitted to by such of the *French* Dominions as pay them to the *States*, was the principal Cause of defeating this Project; since one great Advantage to have been gained by it, was, as before is mentioned, to have hindred the Enemy from erecting their Magazines: and one Article in those Treaties of Contributions is, that the Product of those Countries shall pass free and unmolested. So that the Question was reduced to this short Issue, Whether the *Dutch* should lose this paultry Benefit, or the Common Cause an Advantage of such mighty Importance?

THE Sea being the Element where we might most probably carry on the War with any Advantage to our selves, it was agreed that we should bear five Eighths of the Charge in that Service, and the *Dutch* the other three: And by the Grand Alliance, whatever we or *Holland* should Conquer in the

Spanish West-Indies, was to accrue to the Conquerors. It might therefore have been hoped, that this *Maritime Ally* of ours, would have made up in their Fleet, what they fell short in their Army; but quite otherwise, they never once furnished their Quota either of Ships or Men; or if some few of their Fleet now and then appeared, it was no more than appearing, for they immediately separated to look to their Merchants and protect their Trade. And we may remember very well when these *Guarantees of our Succession*, after having not one Ship for many Months together in the *Mediterranean*, sent that part of their Quota thither, and furnished nothing to us, at the same time that they allarmed us with the Rumour of an Invasion. And last Year, when Sir *James Wishart* was dispatched into *Holland* to expostulate with the *States*, and to desire they would make good their Agreements, in so important a part of the Service; he met with such a Reception as ill became a Republick to give, that lies under so many great Obligations to us; in short, such a one, as those only deserve, who are content to take.

IT hath likewise been no small Inconvenience to us, that the *Dutch* are always slow in paying their Subsidies, by which means the weight and pressure of the Payment lies upon the Queen, as well as the Blame, if Her Majesty be not very exact; nor will even this always content our Allies. For in *July* 1711, the King of *Spain* was paid all his Subsidies to the first of *January* next; nevertheless he hath since complained for want of Mony; and his Secretary threatned, that if we would not further supply his Majesty, he could not answer for what might happen; although King *Charles* had not at that time, one third of the Troops for which he was paid; and even those he had, were neither Paid nor Cloathed.

I SHALL add one Example more, to show how this Prince has treated the Queen, to whom he owes such infinite Obligations. Her Majesty borrowed Two hundred thousand Pounds from the *Genoese*, and sent it to *Barcelona*, for the Payment of the *Spanish* Army: This Mony was to be re-coined into the current Species of *Catalonia*, which by the Allay is lower in Value 25 *l. per Cent.* The Queen expected, as she had Reason,

to have the Benefit of this Re-coinage, offering to apply it All
to the Use of the War; but King *Charles*, instead of consenting
to this, made a Grant of the Coinage to one of his Courtiers;
which put a stop to the Work: And when it was represented,
that the Army would Starve by this Delay, his Majesty only
replied, *Let them Starve!* and would not recal his Grant.

I CANNOT forbear mentioning here another Passage concerning Subsidies, to shew what Opinion Foreigners have
of our Easiness, and how much they reckon themselves Masters
of our Mony, whenever they think fit to call for it. The Queen
was by Agreement to pay Two hundred thousand Crowns a
Year to the *Prussian* Troops, the *States* One hundred thousand,
and the Emperor only Thirty thousand, for Recruiting, which
his Imperial Majesty never paid. Prince *Eugene* happening to
pass by *Berlin*, the Ministers of that Court applied themselves
to him for Redress in this Particular; and his Highness very
frankly promised them, that in Consideration of this Deficiency,
Britain and the *States* should encrease their Subsidies to
Seventy thousand Crowns more between them, and that the
Emperor should be punctual for the time to come: This was
done by that Prince, without any Orders or Power whatsoever. The *Dutch* very reasonably refused consenting to it;
but the *Prussian* Minister here, making his Applications at
our Court, prevailed on us to agree to our Proportion, before
we could hear what Resolution would be taken in *Holland*.
It is therefore to be hoped, that his *Prussian* Majesty, at the
end of this War, will not have the same grievous Cause of
Complaint, which he had at the Close of the last; that his
Military-Chest was emptier by Twenty thousand Crowns, than
at the time that War began.

THE Emperor, as we have already said, was by Stipulation
to furnish Ninety thousand Men against the Common Enemy,
as having no Fleets to maintain, and in Right of his Family
being most concerned in the Success of the War. However,
this Agreement hath been so ill observed, that from the
Beginning of the War to this Day, neither of the two last
Emperors had ever Twenty thousand Men, on their own
Account, in the Common Cause, excepting once in *Italy*; when

the Imperial Court exerted it self in a Point they have much
more at heart than that of gaining *Spain* or the *Indies* to their
Family. When they had succeeded in their Attempts on the
side of *Italy*, and observed our blind Zeal for pushing on the
War at all Adventures, they soon found out the most effectual
Expedient to excuse themselves. They computed easily, that
it would cost them less to make large Presents to one *single
Person*, than to pay an Army, and turn to as good Account.
They thought they could not put their Affairs into better
Hands; and therefore wisely left us to fight their Battles.

BESIDES, it appeared by several Instances, how little the
Emperor regarded his Allies, or the Cause they were engaged
in, when once he thought the Empire it self was secure. 'Tis
known enough, that he might several Times have made a
Peace with his discontented Subjects in *Hungary*, upon Terms
not at all unbefitting either his Dignity or Interest: But he
rather chose to sacrifice the whole Alliance to his private
Passion, by entirely subduing and enslaving a miserable People,
who had but too much Provocation to take up Arms to free
themselves from the Oppressions under which they were
groaning: Yet this must serve as an Excuse for breaking his
Agreement, and diverting so great a Body of Troops, which
might have been employed against *France*.

ANOTHER Instance of the Emperor's Indifference, or
rather Dislike to the Common Cause of the Allies, is the
Business of *Toulon*. This Design was indeed discovered here
at home, by a Person whom every body knows to be the
Creature of a certain *Great Man*, at least as much noted for his
Skill in Gaming as in Politicks, upon the base mercenary End
of getting Mony by Wagers; which was then so common a
Practice, that I remember a Gentleman in Employment, who
having the Curiosity to enquire how Wagers went upon the
Exchange, found some People, deep in the Secret, to have been
concerned in that kind of Traffick, as appeared by Præmiums
named for Towns, which no body but those behind the Cur-
tain could suspect. However, although this Project had gotten
wind by so scandalous a Proceeding, yet *Toulon* might probably
have been taken, if the Emperor had not thought fit, in that

very Juncture, to detach twelve or fifteen thousand Men to seize *Naples*, as an Enterprize that was more his private and immediate Interest. But it was manifest that his Imperial Majesty had no mind to see *Toulon* in Possession of the Allies; for even with these Discouragements the Attempt might have yet succeeded, if Prince *Eugene* had not thought fit to oppose it; which cannot be imputed to his own Judgment, but to some Politick Reasons of his Court. The Duke of *Savoy* was for attacking the Enemy, as soon as our Army arrived; but when the Mareschal *de Thesse*'s Troops were all come up, to pretend to besiege the Place, in the Condition we were at that time, was a Farce and a Jest. Had *Toulon* fallen then into our Hands, the Maritime Power of *France* would, in a great measure, have been destroyed.

BUT a much greater Instance than either of the foregoing, how little the Emperor regarded Us or Our Quarrel, after all we had done to save his Imperial Crown, and to assert the Title of his Brother to the Monarchy of *Spain*, may be brought from the Proceedings of that Court not many Months ago. It was judged, that a War carried on upon the side of *Italy*, would cause a great Diversion of the *French* Forces, wound them in a very tender Part, and facilitate the Progress of our Arms in *Spain*, as well as *Flanders*. It was proposed to the Duke of *Savoy* to make this Diversion; and not only a Diversion during the Summer, but the Winter too, by taking Quarters on this side of the Hills. Only in order to make him willing and able to perform this Work, two Points were to be settled. First, It was necessary to end the Dispute between the Imperial Court, and his Royal Highness; which had no other Foundation, than the Emperor's refusing to make good some Articles of that Treaty, on the Faith of which the Duke engaged in the present War, and for the Execution whereof *Britain* and *Holland* became Guarantees, at the Request of the late Emperor *Leopold*. To remove this Difficulty, the Earl of *Peterborow* was dispatched to *Vienna*, got over some part of those Disputes, to the Satisfaction of the Duke of *Savoy*, and had put the rest in a fair way of being accomodated, at the time the Emperor *Joseph* died. Upon which great Event, the Duke of *Savoy*

took the Resolution of putting himself immediately at the
Head of the Army, though the whole Matter was not finished,
since the Common Cause required his Assistance; and that
until a new Emperor were Elected, it was impossible to make
good the Treaty to Him. In order to enable him, the only
thing he asked was, that he should be reinforced by the
Imperial Court with eight Thousand Men, before the end of
the Campaign. Mr. *Whitworth* was sent to *Vienna* to make this
Proposal, and it is credibly reported, that he was impowered,
rather than fail, to offer forty Thousand Pounds for the
March of those eight Thousand Men, if he found it was want
of Ability, and not Inclination, that hindered the sending
them. But he was so far from succeeding, that it was said,
the Ministers of that Court did not so much as give him an
Opportunity to tempt them with any particular Sums; but cut
off all his Hopes at once, by alleging the Impossibility of
complying with the Queen's Demands, upon any Consideration whatsoever. They could not plead their old Excuse of the
War in *Hungary*, which was then brought to an end: They
had nothing to offer but some general Speculative Reasons,
which it would expose them to repeat; and so, after much
Delay, and many trifling Pretences, they utterly refused so
small and seasonable an Assistance; to the Ruin of a Project
that would have more terrified *France*, and caused a greater
Diversion of their Forces, than a much more numerous Army
in any other Part. Thus, for want of eight Thousand Men, for
whose Winter Campaign the Queen was willing to give forty
Thousand Pounds; and for want of executing the Design
I lately mentioned, of hindring the Enemy from erecting
Magazines, towards which Her Majesty was ready, not only
to bear Her own Proportion, but a Share of that which the
States were obliged to, our Hopes of taking Winter-Quarters
in the North and South Parts of *France* are eluded, and the War
left in that Method, which is like to continue it longest. Can
there an Example be given in the whole Course of this War,
where we have treated the pettiest Prince, with whom we
had to deal, in so contemptuous a manner? Did we ever

once consider what we could afford, or what we were obliged
to, when our Assistance was desired, even while we lay under
immediate Apprehensions of being invaded?

WHEN *Portugal* came, as a Confederate, into the Grand
Alliance, it was stipulated, That the Empire, *England* and
Holland, should each maintain Four thousand Men of their
own Troops in that Kingdom, and pay between them a
Million of Pattacoons to the King of *Portugal*, for the Support
of Twenty eight thousand *Portugueze*; which number of Forty
thousand, was to be the Confederate Army against *Spain* on
the *Portugal* side. This Treaty was ratified by all the Three
Powers. But in a short time after, the Emperor declared himself unable to comply with his part of the Agreement, and so
left the Two thirds upon Us; who very generously undertook
that Burthen, and at the same time Two Thirds of the Subsidies for Maintenance of the *Portugueze* Troops. But neither
is this the worst Part of the Story: For, although the *Dutch*
did indeed send their own particular Quota of Four thousand
Men to *Portugal* (which however they would not agree to,
but upon Condition, that the other Two thirds should be
supplied by us;) yet they never took care to recruit them:
For in the Year 1706. the *Portugueze*, *British* and *Dutch* Forces,
having marched with the Earl of *Galway* into *Castile*, and by
the noble Conduct of that General, being forced to retire
into *Valencia*, it was found necessary to raise a new Army on
the *Portugal* side; where the Queen hath, at several times,
encreased Her Establishment to Ten thousand five hundred
Men, and the *Dutch* never re-placed one single Man, nor paid
one Penny of their Subsidies to *Portugal* in six Years.

THE *Spanish* Army on the side of *Catalonia* is, or ought to
be, about Fifty thousand Men (exclusive of *Portugal*): And
here the War hath been carried on almost entirely at our Cost.
For this whole Army is paid by the Queen, excepting only
seven Battalions and fourteen Squadrons of *Dutch* and *Palatines*;
and even Fifteen hundred of these are likewise in our Pay;
besides the Sums given to King *Charles* for Subsidies and the
Maintenance of his Court. Neither are our Troops at *Gibraltar*
included within this number. And further, we alone have

E

been at all the Charge of Transporting the Forces first sent from *Genoa* to *Barcelona*; and of all the Imperial Recruits from time to time: And have likewise paid vast Sums as Levy-Mony, for every individual Man and Horse so furnished to Recruit, tho' the Horses were scarce worth the Price of Transportation. But this hath been almost the constant Misfortune of our Fleet, during the present War; instead of being employed on some Enterprize for the Good of the Nation, or even for the Protection of our Trade, to be wholly taken up in Transporting Soldiers.

WE have actually Conquered all *Bavaria*, *Ulm*, *Ausburg*, *Landau*, and a great part of *Alsace*, for the Emperor: And by the Troops we have furnished, the Armies we have paid, and the Diversions we have given to the Enemies Forces, have chiefly contributed to the Conquests of *Milan*, *Mantua* and *Mirandola*, and to the Recovery of the Dutchy of *Modena*. The last Emperor drained the Wealth of those Countries into his own Coffers, without encreasing his Troops against *France* by such mighty Acquisitions, or yielding to the most reasonable Requests we have made.

OF the many Towns we have taken for the *Dutch*, we have consented, by the Barrier-Treaty, that all those which were not in Possession of *Spain*, upon the Death of the late Catholick King, shall be part of the *States* Dominions, and that they shall have the Military Power in the most considerable of the rest; which is, in effect, to be the absolute Sovereigns of the whole. And the *Hollanders* have already made such good use of their Time, that, in Conjunction with our General, the Oppressions of *Flanders* are much greater than ever.

AND this Treatment, which we have received from our two principal Allies, hath been pretty well copied by most other Princes in the Confederacy, with whom we have any Dealings. For Instance, Seven *Portugueze* Regiments after the Battle of *Almanza*, went off, with the rest of that broken Army, to *Catalonia*; the King of *Portugal* said, he was not able to pay them, while they were out of his Country; the Queen consented therefore to do it Herself, provided the King would raise as many more to supply their Place. This he engaged to do, but never performed. Notwithstanding which, his Subsidies were constantly paid him by my Lord *Godolphin*, for almost four Years, without any Deduction upon Account of those Seven Regiments; directly contrary to the Seventh Article of our Offensive Alliance with that Crown, where it is agreed, that a Deduction shall be made out of those Subsidies, in Proportion to the number of Men wanting in that Complement, which the King is to maintain. But whatever might have been the Reasons for this Proceeding, it seems they are above the Understanding of the present Lord Treasurer; who not entring into those Refinements, of paying the *publick* Money upon *private* Considerations, hath been so uncourtly as to stop it. This Disappointment, I suppose, hath put the Court of *Lisbon* upon other Expedients of raising the Price of Forage, so as to force us either to lessen our number of Troops, or be at double Expence in maintaining them; and this at a time when their own Product, as well as the Import of Corn, was never greater; And of demanding a Duty upon the Soldiers Cloaths we carry over for those Troops, which have been their sole Defence against an inveterate Enemy; and whose Example might have infused Courage, as well as taught them Discipline, if their Spirits had been capable of receiving either.

IN order to augment our Forces every Year, in the same Proportion as those, for whom we Fight, diminish theirs, we have been obliged to hire Troops from several Princes of the Empire, whose Ministers and Residents here, have perpetually importuned the Court with unreasonable Demands, under which our late Ministers thought fit to be Passive. For those Demands were always backed with a Threat to recall their Soldiers, which was a Thing not to be heard of, because it might *Discontent the Dutch*. In the mean time those Princes never sent their Contingent to the Emperor, as by the Laws of the Empire they are obliged to do, but gave for their Excuse, that we had already hired all they could spare.

BUT if all this be true: If, according to what I have affirmed, we began this War contrary to Reason: If, as the other Party themselves, upon all Occasions, acknowledge, the Success we have had was more than we could reasonably expect: If, after all our Success, we have not made that use of it, which in Reason we ought to have done: If we have made weak and foolish Bargains with our Allies, suffered them tamely to break every Article, even in those Bargains to our Disadvantage, and allowed them to treat us with Insolence and Contempt, at the very Instant when We were gaining Towns, Provinces and Kingdoms for them, at the Price of our Ruin, and without any Prospect of Interest to our selves: If we have consumed all our Strength in attacking the Enemy on the strongest side, where (as the old Duke of *Schomberg* expressed it) *to engage with* France, *was to take a Bull by the Horns*; and left wholly unattempted, that part of the War, which could only enable us to continue or to end it. If all this, I say, be our Case, it is a very obvious Question to ask, by what Motives, or what Management, we are thus become the *Dupes* and *Bubbles* of *Europe?* Sure it cannot be owing to the Stupidity arising from the coldness of our Climate, since those among our Allies, who have given us most Reason to complain, are as far removed from the Sun as our selves.

IF in laying open the real Causes of our present Misery, I am forced to speak with some Freedom, I think it will require no Apology; Reputation is the smallest Sacrifice Those can make us, who have been the Instruments of our Ruin; because it is That, for which in all Probability they have the least Value. So that in exposing the Actions of such Persons, I cannot be said, properly speaking, to do them an Injury. But as it will be some Satisfaction to the People, to know by whom they have been so long abused; so it may be of great use to Us and our Posterity, not to trust the Safety of their Country in the Hands of those, who act by such Principles, and from such Motives.

I HAVE already observed, that when the Counsels of this War were debated in the late King's Time, my Lord *Godolphin* was then so averse from entring into it, that he rather chose to give up his Employment, and tell the King he could serve him no longer. Upon that Prince's Death, although the Grounds of our Quarrel with *France* had received no manner of Addition, yet this Lord thought fit to alter his Sentiments; for the Scene was quite changed; his Lordship, and the Family with whom he was engaged by so complicated an Alliance, were in the highest Credit possible with the Queen: The Treasurer's Staff was ready for his Lordship, the Duke was to Command the Army, and the Dutchess, by her Employments, and the Favour she was possessed of, to be always nearest Her Majesty's Person; by which the whole Power, at Home and Abroad, would be devolved upon that Family. This was a Prospect so very inviting, that, to confess the Truth, it could not be easily withstood by any who have so keen an Appetite for Wealth or Ambition. By an Agreement subsequent to the Grand Alliance, we were to assist the *Dutch* with Forty thousand Men, all to be Commanded by the Duke of *Marlborough*. So that whether this War were prudently begun or not, it is plain, that the true Spring or Motive of it, was the aggrandizing a particular Family, and in short, a War of the *General* and the *Ministry*, and not of the *Prince* or *People*; since those very Persons were against it when they knew the Power, and consequently the Profit, would be in other Hands.

WITH these Measures fell in all that Sett of People, who are called the *Monied Men*; such as had raised vast Sums by Trading with Stocks and Funds, and Lending upon great Interest and Præmiums; whose perpetual Harvest is War, and whose beneficial way of Traffick must very much decline by a Peace.

IN that whole Chain of Encroachments made upon us by the *Dutch*, which I have above deduced, and under those several gross Impositions from other *Powers*, if any one should ask, why our General continued so easy to the last? I know no other way so probable, or indeed so charitable to account for it, as by that unmeasurable Love of Wealth, which his best Friends allow to be his predominant Passion. However, I shall wave any thing that is Personal upon this Subject. I shall say nothing of those great Presents made by several Princes, which the Soldiers used to call Winter Foraging, and said it was better than that of the Summer; of Two and an half *per Cent.* substracted out of all the Subsidies we pay in those Parts, which amounts to no inconsiderable Sum; and lastly, of the grand Perquisites in a long successful War, which are so amicably adjusted between Him and the *States*.

BUT when the War was thus begun, there soon fell in other Incidents here at home, which made the Continuance of it necessary for those who were the chief Advisers. The *Whigs* were at that time out of all Credit or Consideration: The reigning Favourites had always carried what was called the *Tory Principle*, at least, as high as our Constitution could bear: and most others in great Employments, were wholly in the Church-Interest. These last, among whom several were Persons of the greatest Merit, Quality, and Consequence, were not able to endure the many Instances of Pride, Insolence, Avarice and Ambition, which those Favourites began so early to discover, nor to see them presuming to be the sole Dispensers of the Royal Favour. However, their Opposition was to no Purpose; they wrestled with too great a Power, and were soon crushed under it. For, those in Possession finding they could never be quiet in their Usurpations, while others had any Credit, who were at least upon an equal Foot of Merit, began to make Overtures to the discarded *Whigs*, who would be content with any Terms of Accomodation. Thus commenced this *Solemn League and Covenant*, which hath ever since been cultivated with so much Application. The great Traders in Mony were wholly devoted to the *Whigs*, who had first raised them. The Army, the Court, and the Treasury, continued under the old *Despotick* Administration: The *Whigs* were received into Employment, left to manage the Parliament, cry down the Landed Interest, and worry the Church. Mean time, our Allies, who were not ignorant, that all this artificial Structure had no true Foundation in the Hearts of the People, resolved to make their best use of it, as long as it should last. And the General's Credit being raised to a great height at home, by our Success in *Flanders*, the *Dutch* began their gradual Impositions; lessening their Quota's, breaking their Stipulations, Garrisoning the Towns we took for them, without supplying their Troops; with many other Infringements: All which we were forced to submit to, because the General was *made easie*; because the Monied Men at home were fond of the

War; because the *Whigs* were not yet firmly settled; and because that exorbitant degree of Power, which was built upon a supposed Necessity of employing particular Persons, would go off in a Peace. It is needless to add, that the Emperor, and other Princes, followed the Example of the *Dutch*, and succeeded as well, for the same Reasons.

I HAVE here imputed the Continuance of the War to the mutual Indulgence between our General and Allies, wherein they both so well found their Accounts; to the Fears of the *Mony-changers*, lest their *Tables should be overthrown*; to the Designs of the *Whigs*, who apprehended the Loss of their Credit and Employments in a Peace; and to those at home, who held their immoderate Engrossments of Power and Favour, by no other Tenure, than their own Presumption upon the Necessity of Affairs. The Truth of this will appear indisputable, by considering with what Unanimity and Concert these several Parties acted towards that great End.

WHEN the Vote passed in the House of Lords, against any Peace without *Spain* being restored to the *Austrian* Family, the Earl of *Wharton* told the House, That it was indeed impossible and impracticable to recover *Spain*; but however, there were *certain Reasons*, why such a Vote should be made at that time; which Reasons wanted no Explanation: For the General and the Ministry having refused to accept very Advantagious Offers of a Peace, after the Battle of *Ramellies*, were forced to take in a Set of Men, with a previous Bargain, to skreen them from the Consequences of that Miscarriage. And accordingly upon the first succeeding Opportunity, which was that of the Prince of *Denmark*'s Death, the Chief Leaders of the Party were brought into several great Employments.

So when the Queen was no longer able to bear the Tyranny and Insolence of those ungrateful Servants, who as they *wexed the Fatter*, did but *kick the more*; our two great Allies abroad, and our Stock-jobbers at home, took immediate Alarm; applied the nearest way to the Throne, by Memorials and Messages, jointly directing Her Majesty not to change Her Secretary or Treasurer; who for the true Reasons that these officious

Intermedlers demanded their Continuance, ought never to have been admitted into the least Degree of Trust; since what they did was nothing less than betraying the Interest of their Native Country, to those Princes, who in their Turns, were to do what they could to support Them in Power at home.

THUS it plainly appears, that there was a Conspiracy on all sides to go on with those Measures, which must perpetuate the War; and a Conspiracy founded upon the Interest and Ambition of each Party; which begat so firm a Union, that instead of wondring why it lasted so long, I am astonished to think, how it came to be broken. The Prudence, Courage, and Firmness of Her Majesty in all the Steps of that great Change, would, if the Particulars were truly related, make a very shining Part in Her Story: Nor is Her Judgment less to be admired, which directed Her in the Choice of perhaps the only Persons who had Skill, Credit, and Resolution enough to be Her Instruments in overthrowing so many Difficulties.

SOME would pretend to lessen the Merit of this, by telling us, that the Rudeness, the Tyranny, the Oppression, the Ingratitude of the late Favourites towards their Mistress, were no longer to be born. They produce Instances to shew, how Her Majesty was pursued through all Her Retreats, particularly at *Windsor*; where, after the Enemy had possessed themselves of every Inch of Ground, they at last attacked and stormed the Castle, forcing the Queen to fly to an adjoining Cottage, pursuant to the Advice of *Solomon*, who tells us, *It is better to dwell in a corner of the Housetop, than with a brawling Woman in a wide House*. They would have it, that such continued ill Usage was enough to enflame the meekest Spirit: They blame the Favourites in point of Policy, and think it nothing extraordinary, that the Queen should be at an end of Her Patience, and resolve to discard them. But I am of another Opinion, and think their Proceedings were right. For nothing is so apt to break even the bravest Spirits, as a continual Chain of Oppressions: One Injury is best defended by a second, and this by a third. By these Steps, the old *Masters of the Palace* in *France* became *Masters of the Kingdom*; and by these Steps, a *General during Pleasure*, might have grown into a *General for Life*, and a

General for Life into a *King*. So that I still insist upon it as a Wonder, how Her Majesty, thus besieged on all sides, was able to extricate Her self.

HAVING thus mentioned the real Causes, though disguised under specious Pretences, which have so long continued the War; I must beg leave to reason a little, with those Persons who are against any Peace, but what they call a *Good One*; and explain themselves, that no Peace can be *good*, without an entire Restoration of *Spain* to the House of *Austria*. It is to be supposed, that what I am to say upon this Part of the Subject, will have little Influence on those, whose particular Ends or Designs of any sort, lead them to wish the Continuance of the War. I mean the General and our Allies abroad; the Knot of late Favourites at home; the Body of such, as Traffick in Stocks; and lastly, that Set of Factious Politicians, who were so violently bent, at least, upon *Clipping* our Constitution in Church and State. Therefore I shall not apply my self to any of those, but to all others indifferently, whether *Whig* or *Tory*, whose private Interest is best answered by the Welfare of their Country. And if among these there be any, who think we ought to fight on till King *Charles* is quietly settled in the Monarchy of *Spain*, I believe there are several Points, which they have not thoroughly considered.

FOR, First, It is to be observed, that this Resolution against any Peace without *Spain*, is a new Incident, grafted upon the Original Quarrel, by the Intrigues of a Faction among us, who prevailed to give it the Sanction of a Vote in both Houses of Parliament, to justifie those, whose Interest lay in perpetuating the War. And, as this Proceeding was against the Practice of all Princes and States, whose Intentions were fair and honourable; so is it contrary to common Prudence, as well as Justice. I might add, that it was impious too, by presuming to controul Events, which are only in the Hands of God. Ours and the *States* Complaint against *France* and *Spain*, are deduced in each of our Declarations of War, and our Pretensions specified in the *Eighth Article* of the Grand Alliance;

but there is not in any of these, the least mention of demanding *Spain* for the House of *Austria*, or of refusing any Peace without that Condition. Having already made an Extract from both Declarations of War, I shall here give a Translation of the Eighth Article in the Grand Alliance, which will put this Matter out of Dispute.

The Eighth ARTICLE of the
GRAND ALLIANCE.

W HEN *the War is once undertaken, none of the Parties shall have the Liberty to enter upon a Treaty of Peace with the Enemy, but jointly, and in concert with the others. Nor is Peace to be made, without having first obtained a just and reasonable Satisfaction for his* Cesarean *Majesty, and for his Royal Majesty of* Great Britain, *and a particular Security to the Lords the* States-General, *of their Dominions, Provinces, Titles, Navigation, and Commerce, and a sufficient Provision, that the Kingdoms of* France *and* Spain *be never united, or come under the Government of the same Person, or that the same Man may never be King of both Kingdoms; and particularly, that the* French *may never be in Possession of the* Spanish West-Indies; *and that they may not have the liberty of Navigation, for conveniency of Trade, under any Pretence whatsoever, neither directly nor indirectly; except it is agreed, that the Subjects of* Great Britain *and* Holland, *may have full Power to use and enjoy all the same Privileges, Rights, Immunities and Liberties of Commerce, by Land and Sea, in* Spain, *in the* Mediterranean, *and in all the Places and Countries, which the late King of* Spain, *at the time of his Death, was in Possession of, as well in* Europe, *as elsewhere, as they did then use and enjoy; or which the Subjects of both, or each Nation, could use and enjoy, by virtue of any Right, obtained before the Death of the said King of* Spain, *either by Treaties, Conventions, Custom, or any other way whatsoever.*

HERE, we see the Demands intended to be insisted on by the Allies upon any Treaty of Peace, are, a just and reasonable Satisfaction for the Emperor and King of *Great Britain*, a Security to the *States-General* for their Dominions, &c. and a sufficient Provision, that *France* and *Spain* be never united under the same Man, as King of both Kingdoms. The rest relates to the Liberty of Trade and Commerce for Us and the *Dutch*; but not a Syllable of engaging to dispossess the Duke of *Anjou*.

BUT to know how this new Language of *No Peace without Spain*, was first introduced, and at last prevailed among us, we must begin a great deal higher.

IT was the Partition Treaty, which begot the Will in favour of the Duke of *Anjou:* For this naturally led the *Spaniards* to receive a Prince supported by a great Power, whose Interest, as well as Affection, engaged them to preserve that Monarchy entire, rather than to oppose him in favour of another Family, who must expect Assistance from a Number of Confederates, whose principal Members had already disposed of what did not belong to them, and by a previous Treaty parcelled out the Monarchy of *Spain*.

THUS the Duke of *Anjou* got into the full Possession of all the Kingdoms and States belonging to that Monarchy, as well in the old World, as the new. And whatever the House of *Austria* pretended from their Memorials to Us and the *States*, it was at that time but too apparent, that the Inclinations of the *Spaniards* were on the Duke's side.

HOWEVER, a War was resolved, and in order to carry it on with greater Vigor, a Grand Alliance formed, wherein the Ends proposed to be obtained, are plainly and distinctly laid down, as I have already quoted them. It pleased God in the Course of this War, to bless the Armies of the Allies with remarkable Successes; by which we were soon put into a Condition of demanding and expecting such Terms of a Peace, as we proposed to our selves when we began the War. But instead of this, our Victories only served to lead us on to further visionary Prospects; Advantage was taken of the Sanguin Temper, which so many Successes had wrought the Nation up to; new Romantick Views were proposed, and the old, reasonable, sober Design, was forgot.

THIS was the Artifice of those here, who were sure to grow Richer, as the Publick became poorer, and who after the Resolutions, which the two Houses were prevailed upon to make, might have carried on the War with Safety to themselves, till Malt and Land were Mortgaged, till a general Excise were established; and the *dizieme denier* raised, by *Collectors in Red*

Coats. And this was just the Circumstance which it suited their Interests to be in.

THE House of *Austria* approved this Scheme with Reason, since whatever would be obtained by the Blood and Treasure of others, was to accrue to that Family, and they only lent their Name to the Cause.

THE *Dutch* might, perhaps, have grown resty under their Burthen; but Care was likewise taken of That by a *Barrier-Treaty* made with the *States*, which deserveth such Epithets as I care not to bestow: But may perhaps consider it, at a proper Occasion, in a *Discourse* by it self.

BY this Treaty, the Condition of the War, with respect to the *Dutch*, was widely altered: They fought no longer for Security, but for Grandeur; and we, instead of labouring to make them *safe*, must beggar our selves to render them *Formidable*.

WILL any one contend, that if in the Treaty at *Gertruy-denburg*, we could have been satisfied with such Terms of a Peace, as we proposed to our selves by the Grand Alliance, the *French* would not have allowed them? 'Tis plain, they offered many more, and much greater, than ever we thought to insist on, when the War began: And they had reason to grant, as well as we to demand them, since Conditions of Peace do certainly turn upon Events of War. But surely there is some Measure to be observed in this: Those who have defended the Proceedings of our Negotiators at *Gertruydenburg*, dwell very much upon their Zeal and Patience, in endeavouring to work the *French* up to their Demands, but say nothing to justify those Demands, or the Probability, that *France* would ever accept them. Some of the Preliminary Articles were so very Extravagant, that in all Human Probability we could not have obtained them by a successful War of forty Years. One of them was inconsistent with common Reason; wherein the Confederates reserved to themselves full Liberty of demanding, what further Conditions they should think fit; and in the mean time, *France* was to deliver up several of their strongest Towns in a Month. These Articles were very gravely Signed by our Plenipotentiaries, and those of *Holland*, but not by the

French, though it ought to have been done interchangeably; nay they were brought over by the Secretary of the Ambassy; and the Ministers here prevailed on the Queen to execute a Ratification of Articles, which only one Part had Signed: This was an Absurdity in Form, as well as in Reason, because the usual Form of a Ratification is, with a Preamble, shewing, That *whereas Our Ministers and those of the Allies, and of the Enemy, have Signed,* &c. *We Ratify,* &c. The Person who brought over the Articles, said in all Companies, (and perhaps believed) that it was a Pity, we had not demanded more, for the *French* were in a Disposition to refuse us nothing we would ask. One of our Plenipotentiaries affected to have the same Concern, and particularly, that we had not obtained some further Security for the Empire on the *Upper Rhine*.

WHAT could be the Design of all this Grimace, but to amuse the People, and raise Stocks for their Friends in the Secret, to Sell to Advantage? I have too great a Respect for the Abilities of those, who acted in this Negotiation, to believe they hoped for any other Issue from it, than what we found by the Event. Give me leave to suppose the continuance of the War was the Thing at Heart, among those in Power, both Abroad, and at Home, and then I can easily shew the Consistency of their Proceedings; otherwise they are wholly unaccountable and absurd. Did those, who insisted on such wild Demands, ever sincerely intend a Peace? Did they really think that going on with the War was more eligible for their Country, than the least Abatement of those Conditions? Was the smallest of them worth Six Millions a Year, and an Hundred thousand Men's Lives? Was there no way to provide for the Safety of *Britain*, or the Security of its Trade, but by the *French* King's turning his own Arms to beat his Grandson out of *Spain*? If these able Statesmen were so truly concerned for our Trade, which they made the Pretence of the War's Beginning, as well as Continuance, why did they so neglect it in those very Preliminaries, where the Enemy made so many Concessions, and where all that related to the Advantage of *Holland*, or the other Confederates, was expresly settled? But whatever concerned us, was to be left to a general

Treaty; no Tariff agreed on with *France* or the *Low Countries*, only the *Schelde* was to remain shut, which ruins our Commerce with *Antwerp*. Our Trade with *Spain* was referred the same way; but this they will pretend to be of no Consequence, because that Kingdom was to be under the House of *Austria*; and we had already made a Treaty with King *Charles*. I have indeed heard of a Treaty made by Mr. *Stanhope*, with that Prince, for settling our Commerce with *Spain:* But whatever it were, there was another between Us and *Holland*, which went Hand in Hand with it, I mean that of *Barrier*, wherein a Clause was inserted, by which all Advantages proposed for *Britain*, are to be in common with *Holland*.

ANOTHER Point which, I doubt, those have not considered, who are against any Peace without *Spain*, is, that the Face of Affairs in *Christendom*, since the Emperor's Death, hath been very much changed. By this Accident the Views and Interests of several Princes and States in the Alliance, have taken a new Turn, and I believe, it will be found that Ours ought to do so too. We have sufficiently blundered once already, by changing our Measures with regard to a Peace, while our Affairs continued in the same Posture; and it will be too much in Conscience to blunder again by *not* changing the first, when the others are so much altered.

To have a Prince of the *Austrian* Family on the Throne of *Spain*, is undoubtedly more desirable than one of the House of *Bourbon*; but to have the Empire and *Spanish* Monarchy united in the same Person, is a dreadful Consideration, and directly opposite to that wise Principle, on which the Eighth Article of the Grand Alliance is founded*.

To this perhaps it will be objected, that the indolent Character of the *Austrian* Princes, the wretched Oeconomy of that Government, the want of a Naval Force, the remote distance of their several Territories from each other, would

---

* *We and* Holland, *as well as* Portugal, *were so apprehensive of this, that, by the* 25*th Article of the Offensive Alliance, his* Portugueze *Majesty was not to acknowledge the Arch-Duke for King of* Spain, *till the two late Emperors had made a Cession to* Charles *of the said Monarchy.*

never suffer an Emperor, though at the same time King of *Spain*, to become Formidable: On the contrary, that his Dependance must continually be on *Great Britain*; and the Advantages of Trade, by a Peace founded upon that Condition, would soon make us Amends for all the Expences of the War.

IN Answer to this, Let us consider the Circumstances we must be in, before such a Peace could be obtained, if it were at all practicable. We must become not only Poor for the present, but reduced by further Mortgages to a state of Beggary, for endless Years to come. Compare such a weak Condition as this with so great an Accession of Strength to *Austria*, and then determine how much an Emperor, in such a State of Affairs, would either fear or need *Britain*.

CONSIDER, that the Comparison is not formed between a Prince of the House of *Austria*, Emperor and King of *Spain*, and between a Prince of the *Bourbon* Family, King of *France* and *Spain*; but between a Prince of the latter only King of *Spain*, and one of the former uniting both Crowns in his own Person.

WHAT Returns of Gratitude can we expect, when we are no longer wanted? Has all that we have hitherto done for the Imperial Family been taken as a Favour, or only received as the Due of the *Augustissima Casa?*

WILL the House of *Austria* yield the least Acre of Land, the least Article of strained and even usurped Prerogative, to resettle the Minds of those Princes in the Alliance, who are alarmed at the Consequences of this Turn of Affairs, occasioned by the Emperor's Death? We are assured it never will. Do we then imagine, that those Princes, who dread the overgrown Power of the *Austrian*, as much as that of the *Bourbon* Family, will continue in our Alliance, upon a System contrary to that which they engaged with us upon? For instance; What can the Duke of *Savoy* expect in such a Case? Will he have any Choice left him but that of being a Slave and a Frontier to *France*; or a *Vassal*, in the utmost Extent of the Word, to the Imperial Court? Will he not therefore, of the two Evils choose the least; by submitting to a Master, who has no immediate Claim upon Him, and to whose Family he is nearly allied;

rather than to another, who hath already revived several Claims upon him, and threatens to revive more?

NOR are the *Dutch* more inclined than the rest of *Europe*, that the *Empire* and *Spain* should be united in King *Charles*, whatever they may now pretend. *On the contrary, 'tis known to several Persons, that upon the Death of the late Emperor* Joseph, *the* States *resolved, that those two Powers should not be joined in the same Person*; And this they determined as a fundamental Maxim, by which they intended to proceed. So that *Spain* was first given up by *Them*; and since they maintain no Troops in that Kingdom, it should seem, that they understand the Duke of *Anjou* to be lawful Monarch.

THIRDLY, Those who are against any Peace without *Spain*, if they be such as no way find their private Account by the War, may perhaps change their Sentiments, if they will reflect a little upon our present Condition.

I HAD two Reasons for not sooner publishing this Discourse: The first was, Because I would give way to others, who might argue very well upon the same Subject, from general Topicks and Reason, though they might be ignorant of several Facts, which I had the Opportunity to know. The Second was, Because I found it would be necessary, in the course of this Argument, to say something of the State to which this War hath reduced us: At the same time I knew, that such a Discovery ought to be made as late as possible, and at another Juncture would not only be very indiscreet, but might perhaps be dangerous.

IT is the Folly of too many, to mistake the Eccho of a *London* Coffee-house for the Voice of the Kingdom. The City Coffee-houses have been for some Years filled with People, whose Fortunes depend upon the *Bank, East-India*, or some other Stock: Every new Fund to these, is like a new Mortgage to an Usurer, whose Compassion for a young Heir is exactly the same with that of a Stockjobber to the Landed Gentry. At the Court-End of the Town, the like Places of Resort are frequented either by Men out of Place, and consequently Enemies to the Present Ministry, or by Officers of the Army:

F

No wonder then, if the general Cry, in all such Meetings, be against any Peace either *with* Spain, or *without*; which, in other Words, is no more than this, That discontented Men desire another Change of Ministry; that Soldiers would be glad to keep their Commissions; and, that the Creditors have Mony still, and would have the Debtors borrow on at the old extorting Rates, while they have any Security to give.

Now, to give the most ignorant Reader some Idea of our present Circumstances, without troubling him or my self with Computations in form: Every body knows, that our Land and Malt Tax amount annually to about Two Millions and an half. All other Branches of the Revenue are mortgaged to pay Interest, for what we have already borrowed. The yearly Charge of the War is usually about Six Millions; to make up which Sum, we are forced to take up, on the Credit of new Funds, about Three Millions and an half. This last Year the computed Charge of the War came to above a Million more, than all the Funds the Parliament could contrive would pay Interest for; and so we have been forced to divide a Deficiency of Twelve hundred thousand Pounds among the several Branches of our Expence. This is a Demonstration, that if the War lasts another Campaign, it will be impossible to find Funds for supplying it, without mortgaging the Malt Tax, or by some other Method equally desperate.

If the Peace be made this Winter, we are then to consider, what Circumstances we shall be in towards paying a Debt of about Fifty Millions, which is a fourth Part of the Purchase of the whole Island, if it were to be Sold.

Towards clearing our selves of this monstrous Incumbrance, some of these Annuities will expire or pay off the Principal in Thirty, Forty, or an Hundred Years; the Bulk of the Debt must be lessened gradually by the best Management we can, out of what will remain of the Land and Malt Taxes, after paying Guards and Garrisons, and maintaining and supplying our Fleet in the time of Peace. I have not Skill enough to compute what will be left, after these necessary Charges, towards annually clearing so vast a Debt; but believe it must be very little: However, it is plain that both these

Taxes must be continued, as well for supporting the Government, as because we have no other Means for paying off the Principal. And so likewise must all the other Funds remain for paying the Interest. How long a time this must require, how steddy an Administration, and how undisturbed a state of Affairs, both at Home and Abroad, let others determine.

HOWEVER, some People think all this very reasonable, and that since the Struggle hath been for Peace and Safety, Posterity, who is to partake the Benefit, ought to share in the Expence: As if at the breaking out of this War there had been such a Conjuncture of Affairs, as never happened before, nor would ever happen again. 'Tis wonderful, that our Ancestors, in all their Wars, should never fall under such a Necessity; that we meet no Examples of it, in *Greece* and *Rome*; that no other Nation in *Europe* ever knew any thing like it, except *Spain*, about an Hundred and twenty Years ago; which they drew upon themselves, by their own Folly, and have suffered for it ever since: No doubt, we shall teach Posterity Wisdom, but they will be apt to think the Purchase too dear; and I wish they may stand to the Bargain we have made in their Names.

'TIS easy to entail Debts on succeeding Ages, and to hope they will be able and willing to pay them; but how to insure Peace for any Term of Years, is difficult enough to apprehend. Will Human Nature ever cease to have the same Passions? Princes to entertain Designs of Interest or Ambition, and Occasions of Quarrel to arise? May not we Ourselves, by the variety of Events and Incidents which happen in the World, be under a necessity of recovering Towns out of the very Hands of those, for whom we are now ruining Our Country to Take them? Neither can it be said, that those *States*, with whom we may probably differ, will be in as bad a Condition as Ourselves; for, by the Circumstances of our Situation, and the Impositions of our Allies, we are more exhausted, than either they or the Enemy; and by the Nature of our Government, the Corruption of our Manners, and the Opposition of Factions, we shall be more slow in recovering.

IT will, no doubt, be a mighty Comfort to our Grand-children, when they see a few Rags hang up in *Westminster-*

Hall, which cost an hundred Millions, whereof they are paying the Arrears, and boasting, as Beggars do, that their Grandfathers were Rich and Great.

I HAVE often reflected on that mistaken Notion of Credit, so boasted of by the Advocates of the late Ministry: Was not all that Credit built upon Funds, raised by the Landed Men, whom they so much hate and despise? Are not the greatest part of those Funds raised from the Growth and Product of Land? Must not the whole Debt be entirely paid, and our Fleets and Garrisons be maintained, by the Land and Malt-Tax, after a Peace? If they call it Credit to run Ten Millions in Debt, without Parliamentary Security, by which the Publick is defrauded of almost half, I must think such Credit to be dangerous, illegal, and perhaps treasonable. Neither hath any thing gone further to ruin the Nation, than their boasted Credit. For my own part, when I saw this false Credit sink, upon the Change of the Ministry, I was singular enough to conceive it a good Omen. It seemed, as if the young extravagant Heir had got a new Steward, and was resolved to look into his Estate before things grew desperate, which made the Usurers forbear feeding him with Mony, as they used to do.

SINCE the Monied Men are so fond of War, I should be glad, they would furnish out one Campaign at their own Charge: It is not above six or seven Millions; and I dare engage to make it out, that when they have done this, instead of contributing equal to the Landed Men, they will have their full Principal and Interest, at 6 *per Cent*. remaining of all the Money they ever lent to the Government.

WITHOUT this Resource, or some other equally miraculous, it is impossible for us to continue the War upon the same Foot. I have already observed, that the last Funds of Interest fell short above a Million, though the Persons most conversant in Ways and Means employed their utmost Invention; so that of necessity we must be still more defective next Campaign. But, perhaps our Allies will make up this Deficiency on our side, by greater Efforts on their own. Quite the contrary; both the Emperor and *Holland* failed this Year in several Articles; and signified to us, some time ago, that they cannot keep up to the same Proportions in the next. We have gained a noble Barrier for the latter, and they have nothing more to demand or desire. The Emperor, however sanguin he may now affect to appear, will, I suppose, be satisfied with *Naples*, *Sicily*, *Milan*, and his other Acquisitions, rather than engage in a long hopeless War, for the Recovery of *Spain*, to which his Allies the *Dutch* will neither give their Assistance nor Consent. So that since we have done their Business; since they have no further Service for our Arms, and we have no more Money to give them: And lastly, since we neither desire any Recompence, nor expect any Thanks, we ought, in pity, to be dismissed, and have leave to shift for ourselves. They are ripe for a Peace, to enjoy and cultivate what we have conquered for them; and so are we, to recover, if possible, the Effects of their Hardships upon Us. The first Overtures from *France*, are made to *England*, upon safe and honourable Terms: We who bore the Burthen of the War, ought, in reason, to have the greatest share in making the Peace. If we do not hearken to a Peace, others certainly will; and get the Advantage of us there, as they have done in the War. We know the *Dutch* have perpetually threatned us, that they would enter into separate Measures of a Peace; and by the Strength of that Argument, as well as by *other Powerful Motives*, prevailed on those, who were then at the Helm, to comply with them on any Terms, rather than put an end to a War, which every Year brought them such great Accessions to their Wealth and Power. Whoever falls off, a Peace will follow; and then we must be content with such Conditions, as our Allies, out of their great Concern for our Safety and Interest, will please to choose. They have no further occasion for Fighting; they have gained their Point, and they now tell us, it is *our War*; so that in common Justice, it ought to be *our Peace*.

ALL we can propose, by the desperate Steps of pawning our Land or Malt-Tax, or erecting a General Excise, is only to raise a Fund of Interest, for running us annually four Millions further in Debt, without any Prospect of ending the War so well, as we can do at present: And when we have sunk the only un-engaged Revenues we had left, our Incumbrances must of necessity remain perpetual.

WE have hitherto lived upon *Expedients*, which in time will certainly destroy any Constitution, whether Civil or Natural, and there was no Country in *Christendom* had less Occasion for them, than ours. We have dieted a Healthy Body into a Consumption, by plying it with Physick, instead of Food; Art will help us no longer; and if we cannot recover by letting the Remains of Nature work, we must inevitably die.

WHAT Arts have been used to possess the People with a *strong Delusion*, that *Britain* must infallibly be ruined, without the Recovery of *Spain* to the House of *Austria?* Making the Safety of a great and powerful Kingdom, as ours was then, to depend upon an Event, which, even after a War of miraculous Successes, proves impracticable. As if Princes and Great Ministers could find no way of settling the Publick Tranquility, without changing the Possessions of Kingdoms, and forcing Sovereigns upon a People against their Inclinations. Is there no Security for the Island of *Britain*, unless a King of *Spain* be Dethroned by the Hands of his Grandfather? Has the Enemy no Cautionary Towns and Sea-Ports, to give us for securing Trade? Can he not deliver us Possession of such Places, as would put him in a worse Condition, whenever he should perfidiously renew the War? The present King of *France* has but few Years to live, by the Course of Nature, and, doubtless, would desire to end his Days in Peace: Grandfathers in private Families are not observed to have great Influence on their Grandsons, and I believe they have much less among Princes. However, when the Authority of a Parent is gone, is it likely that *Philip* will be directed by a Brother, against his own Interest, and that of his Subjects? Have not those two Realms their separate Maxims of Policy, which must operate in Times of Peace? These at least are Probabilities, and cheaper by six Millions a Year than recovering *Spain*, or continuing the War, both which seem absolutely impossible.

BUT the common Question is, If we must now Surrender

Spain, what have we been Fighting for all this while? The Answer is ready; We have been Fighting for the Ruin of the Publick Interest, and the Advancement of a Private. We have been fighting to raise the Wealth and Grandeur of a particular Family; to enrich Usurers and Stock-jobbers; and to cultivate the pernicious Designs of a Faction, by destroying the Landed-Interest. The Nation begins now to think these *Blessings* are not worth Fighting for any longer, and therefore desires a Peace.

BUT the Advocates on the other side cry out, that we might have had a better Peace, than is now in Agitation, above two Years ago. Supposing this to be true, I do assert, that by parity of Reason we must expect one just so much worse, about two Years hence. If those in Power could then have given us a better Peace, more is their Infamy and Guilt, that they did it not; why did they insist upon Conditions, which they were certain would never be granted? We allow it was in their Power to have put a good End to the War, and left the Nation in some hope of recovering it self. And this is what we charge them with as answerable to God, their Country, and Posterity, that the bleeding Condition of their Fellow-Subjects, was a Feather in the Balance with their private Ends.

WHEN we offer to lament the heavy Debts and Poverty of the Nation, 'tis pleasant to hear some Men answer all that can be said, by crying up the Power of *England*, the Courage of *England*, the inexhaustible Riches of *England*. I have heard a Man very sanguine upon this Subject, with a good Employment for Life, and a Hundred thousand Pounds in the Funds, bidding us *Take Courage*, and *Warranting, that all would go well.* This is the Style of Men at Ease, *who lay the heavy Burthens upon others, which they will not touch with one of their Fingers.* I have known some People such ill Computers, as to imagine the many Millions in Stocks and Annuities, are so much real Wealth in the Nation; whereas every Farthing of it is entirely lost to us, scattered in *Holland*, *Germany*, and *Spain*; and the Landed-Men, who now pay the Interest, must at last pay the Principal.

FOURTHLY, Those who are against any Peace without *Spain*, have, I doubt, been ill informed, as to the low Condition of *France*, and the mighty Consequences of our Successes. As to the first, it must be confessed, that after the Battle of *Ramellies* the *French* were so discouraged with their frequent Losses, and so impatient for a Peace, that their King was resolved to comply on any reasonable Terms. But when his Subjects were informed of our exorbitant Demands, they grew jealous of his Honour, and were unanimous to assist him in continuing the War at any hazard, rather than submit. This fully restored his Authority; and the Supplies he hath received from the *Spanish West-Indies*, which in all are computed, since the War, to amount to Four hundred Millions of Livres, (and all in *Specie*) have enabled him to pay his Troops. Besides, the Money is spent in his own Country; and he hath since waged War in the most thrifty manner, by acting on the Defensive, compounding with us every Campaign for a Town, which costs us fifty times more than it is worth, either as to the Value, or the Consequences. Then he is at no Charge of a Fleet, further than providing Privateers, wherewith his Subjects carry on a Piratical War at their own Expence, and he shares in the Profit; which hath been very considerable to *France*, and of infinite Disadvantage to us, not only by the perpetual Losses we have suffered to an immense Value, but by the general Discouragement of Trade, on which we so much depend. All this considered, with the Circumstances of that Government, where the Prince is Master of the Lives and Fortunes of so mighty a Kingdom, shews that Monarch to be not so sunk in his Affairs, as we have imagined, and have long flattered Our selves with the Hopes of. For an absolute Government may endure a long War, but it hath generally been ruinous to Free Countries.

THOSE who are against *any Peace without Spain*, seem likewise to have been mistaken in judging our Victories, and other Successes, to have been of greater Consequence, than they really were.

WHEN our Armies take a Town in *Flanders*, the *Dutch* are immediately put into *Possession*, and we at home make *Bonfires*.

I have sometimes pitied the deluded People, to see them squandring away their Fewel to so little purpose. For Example, What is it to Us that *Bouchain* is taken, about which the Warlike Politicians of the Coffee-House make such a Clutter? What though the Garrison surrendered Prisoners of War, and in sight of the Enemy? We are not now in a Condition to be fed with Points of Honour. What Advantage have We, but that of spending three or four Millions more to get another Town for the States, which may open them a new Country for *Contributions*, and encrease the Perquisites of the General?

IN that War of Ten Years, under the late King, when our Commanders and Soldiers were raw and unexperienced, in comparison of what they are at present, we lost Battles and Towns, as well as we gained them of late, since those Gentlemen have better learned their Trade; yet we bore up then, as the *French* do now: Nor was there any thing decisive in their Successes: They grew weary, as well as we, and at last consented to a Peace, under which we might have been happy enough, if it had not been followed by that wise *Treaty* of *Partition*, which revived the Flame, that hath lasted ever since. I see nothing else in the modern way of making War, but that the Side, which can hold out longest, will end it with most Advantage. In such a close Country as *Flanders*, where it is carried on by Sieges, the Army, that acts offensively, is at a much greater Expence of Men and Mony; and there is hardly a Town taken in the common Forms, where the Besiegers have not the worse of the Bargain. I never yet knew a Soldier, who would not affirm, That any Town might be Taken, if you were content to be at the Charge. If you will count upon sacrificing so much Blood and Treasure, the rest is all a regular, established Method, which cannot fail. When the King of *France*, in the Times of his Grandeur, sat down before a Town, his Generals and Engineers would often fix the Day when it should Surrender. The Enemy, sensible of all this, hath for some Years past avoided a Battle, where he hath so ill succeeded, and taken a surer way to consume us, by letting our Courage evaporate against Stones and Rubbish, and sacrificing a single Town to a Campaign, which he can so much better afford to Lose, than we to Take.

LASTLY, Those who are so violent against *any Peace*, without *Spain* being restored to the House of *Austria*, have not, I believe, cast their Eye upon a Cloud gathering in the North, which we have helped to raise, and may quickly break in a Storm upon our Heads.

THE Northern War hath been on Foot, almost ever since our Breach with *France*: The Success of it various; but one Effect to be apprehended was always the same, that sooner or later it would involve us in its Consequences, and that, whenever this happened, let our Success be never so great against *France*, from that Moment *France* would have the Advantage.

BY our Guaranty of the Treaty of *Travendall*, we were obliged to hinder the King of *Denmark* from engaging in a War with *Sueden*. It was at that time understood by all Parties, and so declared, even by the *British* Ministers, that this Engagement especially regarded *Denmark*'s not assisting King *Augustus*. But, however, if this had not been so, yet our Obligation to *Sueden* stood in Force, by virtue of former Treaties with that Crown, which were all revived and confirmed by a subsequent one, concluded at the *Hague* by Sir *Joseph William-son* and Monsieur *Lilienroot*, about the latter end of the late King's Reign.

HOWEVER, the War in the North proceeded, and our not assisting *Sueden*, was at least as well excused by the War, which we were entangled in, as his not contributing his Contingent to the Empire, whereof he is a Member, was excused by the Pressures he lay under, having a Confederacy to deal with.

IN this War the King of *Sueden* was Victorious; and what Dangers were we not then exposed to? What Fears were we not in? He Marched into *Saxony*, and if he had really been in the *French* Interest, might at once have put us under the greatest Difficulties. But the Torrent turned another way, and he contented himself with imposing on his Enemy the Treaty of *Alt Rastadt*; by which King *Augustus* makes an absolute Cession of the Crown of *Poland*, renounces any Title to it, acknowledges *Stanislaus*; and then, both he and the King of *Sueden*, join in desiring the Guaranty of *England* and *Holland*. The Queen did, indeed, not give this Guaranty in Form; but, as a Step towards it, the Title of *King* was given to *Stanislaus*, by a Letter from Her Majesty; and the strongest Assurances were made to the *Suedish* Minister, in Her Majesty's Name and in a Committee of Council, that the Guaranty should speedily be granted; and that in the mean while, it was the same thing as if the Forms were passed.

IN 1708, King *Augustus* made the Campaign in *Flanders*; what Measures he might at that time take, or of *what Nature* the Arguments might be that he made use of, is not known: But immediately after he breaks through all he had done, marches into *Poland*, and re-assumes the Crown.

AFTER this we apprehended, that the Peace of the Empire might be endangered; and therefore entered into an Act of Guaranty for the Neutrality of it. The King of *Sueden* refused, upon several Accounts, to submit to the Terms of this Treaty; particularly, because we went out of the Empire to cover *Poland* and *Jutland*, but did not go out of it to cover the Territories of *Sueden*.

LET us therefore consider, what is our Case at present. If the King of *Sueden* returns, and gets the better, he will think himself under no Obligation of having any Regard to the Interests of the Allies; but will naturally pursue, according to his own Expression, *His Enemy, wherever he finds him*. In this Case the *Corps* of the Neutrality is obliged to oppose him, and so we are engaged in a second War, before the first is ended.

IF the Northern Confederates succeed against *Sueden*, how shall we be able to preserve the Balance of Power in the North, so essential to our Trade, as well as in many other Respects? What will become of that great Support of the *Protestant Interest* in *Germany*, which is the Footing that the *Suedes* now have in the Empire? Or, who shall answer that these Princes, after they have settled the North to their Minds, may not take a fancy to look Southward, and make our Peace with *France* according to their own Schemes?

AND lastly, if the King of *Prussia*, the Elector of *Hanover*, and other Princes whose Dominions lie contiguous, are forced to draw from those Armies which act against *France*; we must live in hourly Expectation of having those Troops recalled, which they now leave with us; and this Recal may happen in the midst of a Siege, or on the Eve of a Battel. Is it therefore our Interest, to toil on in a ruinous War, for an impracticable End, till one of these Cases shall happen, or to get under shelter before the Storm?

THERE is no doubt, but the present Ministry (provided they could get over the Obligations of Honour and Conscience) might find their Advantage in advising the Continuance of the War, as well as the last did, though not in the same Degree, after the Kingdom has been so much exhausted. They might prolong it till the Parliament would desire a Peace; and in the mean time leave them in full Possession of Power. Therefore it is plain, that their Proceedings at present, are meant to serve their Country, directly against their private Interest; whatever Clamor may be raised by those, who for the vilest Ends, would remove Heaven and Earth to oppose their Measures. But they think it infinitely better, to accept such Terms as will secure our Trade, find a sufficient Barrier for the *States*, give *Reasonable Satisfaction* to the Emperor, and restore the Tranquility of *Europe*, though without adding *Spain* to the Empire: Rather than go on in a languishing way, upon the vain Expectation of some improbable Turn, for the Recovery of that Monarchy out of the *Bourbon* Family; and at last be forced to a worse Peace, by some of the Allies falling off, upon our utter Inability to continue the War.

POSTSCRIPT:

I Have in this Edition explained three or four Lines in the 38th Page,* which mentions the *Succession*, to take off, if possible, all manner of Cavil; though, at the same time, I cannot but observe, how ready the Adverse Party is to make use of any Objections, even such as destroy their own Principles. I put a distant Case of the possibility that our *Succession*, through extream Necessity, might be changed by the Legislature, in future Ages; and it is pleasant to hear those People quarrelling at this, who profess themselves for changing it as often as they please, and that even without the Consent of the entire Legislature.

I HAVE just seen a Paper, called, *An Answer to the Conduct*, &c. I am told several Others are preparing: I faithfully promise, that whatever Objections of Moment I can find in any of them, shall be fully answered in a Paragraph at the end of the Preface, in the next Edition of this Discourse.

FINIS.

* See above, p. 27, ll. 25–28.

SOME ADVICE
TO THE OCTOBER CLUB

SOME
ADVICE

Humbly Offer'd to the

MEMBERS

OF THE

OCTOBER CLUB,

IN A

LETTER

FROM A

Perſon of Honour.

LONDON,

Printed for *John Morphew,* near *Stationers-Hall,* 1712.   Price 2 *d.*

G

SOME
ADVICE, &c.

Gentlemen,

SINCE the first Institution of your Society, I have always thought you capable of the greatest Things. Such a number of Persons, Members of Parliament, true Lovers of our Constitution in Church and State, meeting at certain times, and mixing Business and Conversation together, without the forms and Constraint necessary to be observed in Publick Assemblies, must very much improve each others Understanding, correct and fix your Judgment, and prepare your selves against any Designs of the opposite Party. Upon the opening of this Session, an Incident hath happen'd, to provide against the Consequences whereof will require your utmost Vigilance and Application. All this last Summer the Enemy was working under Ground, and laying their Train; they gradually became more frequent and bold in their Pamphlets and Papers, while those on our side were drop'd, as if we had no farther occasion for them. Some time before an Opportunity fell into their Hands, which they have cultivated ever since; and thereby have endeavoured, in some sort, to turn those Arts against us, which had been so effectually employ'd to their Ruin: A plain Demonstration of their superior Skill at Intrigue; to make a Stratagem succeed a second time, and this even against those who first try'd it upon Them. I know not whether this Opportunity I have mentioned could have been prevented by any Care, without straining a very *tender Point*, which those chiefly concern'd avoided by all means, because it might seem a Counterpart of what they had so much condemn'd in their *Predecessors*. Though it is certain the two Cases were widely different; and if Policy had once got the better of good Nature, all had been safe, for there was no other Danger in view: But the Consequences of this were foreseen from the beginning, and those who *kept the Watch* had early warning of it. It would have been a Master-Piece of Prudence, in this Case, to have made a *Friend* of an *Enemy*. But whether that were possible to be compass'd, or whether it were ever attempted, is now too late to enquire. All Accommodation was render'd desperate, by an unlucky Proceeding some Months ago at *Windsor*, which was a Declaration of War too frank and generous for that Situation of Affairs, and, I am told, was not approved by a certain great Minister. It was obvious to suppose, that in a Particular where the Honour and Interest of a *Husband* were so closely united with those of a *Wife*, he might be sure of her utmost Endeavours for his Protection, though she neither lov'd nor esteem'd him. The Danger of losing Power, Favour, Profit, and a Shelter from *Domestick Tyranny*, were strong Incitements to stir up a working Brain, *early* practis'd in all the Arts of Intriguing. Neither is it safe to count upon the Weakness of any Man's Understanding, who is thoroughly possess'd with the Spirit of Revenge to sharpen his Invention: Nothing else is required besides *Obsequiousness* and *Assiduity*, which as they are often the Talents of those who have no better, so they are apt to make Impressions upon the *best and greatest Minds*.

It was no small Advantage to the *designing Party*, that since the Adventure at *Windsor*, the *Person on whom we so much depend*, was long absent by Sickness; which hinder'd him from pursuing those Measures, that Ministers are in Prudence forc'd to take, to defend their Country and themselves against an irritated Faction. The *Negotiators* on the other side, improv'd this favourable Conjuncture to the utmost; and by an unparallel'd Boldness, accompany'd with many Falshoods, persuaded certain Lords, who were already in the same Principle, but were afraid of making a wrong Step, lest it should *lead them out of their Coaches into the Dirt*, that Voting, in appearance, against the Court, would be the safest Course, to avoid the danger they most apprehended, which was that of losing their Pensions; and their Opinions, when produced, would, by seemingly contradicting their Interest, have an appearance of Virtue into the bargain. This, with some Arguments of more *immediate Power*, went far in producing that strange unexpected Turn we have so lately seen, and from which our Adversaries reckon'd upon such wonderful Effects: and some of them, particularly my Lord Chief Justice, began to act as if all were already in their Power.

BUT, though the more immediate Causes of this Desertion were what I have above related, yet I am apt to think, it would hardly have been attempted, or at least not have succeeded, but for a prevailing Opinion, that the Church Party, and the Ministers, had different Views, or at least were not so firmly united as they ought to have been. It was commonly said, and I suppose not without some Ground of Truth, that many Gentlemen of your Club were discontented to find so *little done*; that they thought it look'd as if People were *not in earnest*; that they expected to see a *thorough Change*, with respect to Employments; and though every Man could not be provided for, yet when all Places were filled with Persons of good Principles, there would be fewer Complaints, and less danger from the other Party; that this Change was hop'd for all last Summer, and even to the Opening of the Session, yet nothing done. On the other Hand, it was urged by some in favour of the Ministry, that it was impossible to find Employments for one *Pretender* in twenty, and therefore, in gratifying one, nineteen would be disoblig'd; but while all had leave to hope, they would all endeavour to deserve: But this again was esteem'd a very shallow Policy, which was too easily seen through, must soon come to an end, and would cause a general Discontent; with twenty other Objections, to which it was liable: And indeed, considering the short Life of Ministrys in our Climate, it was with some Reason thought a little hard, that those for whom any Employment was intended, should, by such a Delay, be probably deprived of half their Benefit; not to mention, that a Ministry is best confirm'd, when all inferior Officers are in its Interest.

I HAVE set this Cause of Complaint in the strongest Light, tho' my Design is to endeavour that it should have no manner of Weight with you, as I am confident our Adversaries counted upon, and do still expect to find mighty Advantages by it.

BUT it is necessary to say something to this Objection, which in all Appearance lies so hard upon the present Ministry. What shall I offer upon so tender a Point? How shall I convey an Answer that none will apprehend except those for whom I intend it? I have often pitied the Condition of great Ministers upon several Accounts, but never so much upon any, as when their Duty obliges them to bear the Blame and Envy of Actions, for which they will not be answerable in the next World, tho' they dare not convince the present, 'till it is too late. This Letter is sent you, *Gentlemen*, from no mean Hand, nor from a Person uninformed, though for the rest as little concerned in Point of Interest for any change of Ministry, as most others of his Fellow-Subjects. I may therefore assume so much to my self, as to desire you will depend upon it, that a short time will make manifest, how little the Defect you complain of, ought to lye at *that Door*, where your Enemies would be glad to see you place it. The wisest Man, who is not very near the Spring of Affairs, but views them only in their Issues and Events, will be apt to fix Applauses and Reproaches in the wrong Place; which is the true Cause of a Weakness that I never yet knew Great Ministers without, I mean their being deaf to all Advice; for if a Person of the best Understanding offers his Opinion in a Point where he is not Master of all the Circumstances, (which perhaps are not to be told) 'tis an hundred to one, that he runs into an Absurdity: From whence it is that Ministers falsly conclude themselves to be equally Wiser than others in general Things, where the common Reason of Mankind ought to be the Judge; and is probably less byassed than theirs. I have known a Great Man of excellent Parts, blindly pursue a Point of no Importance, against the Advice of every Friend he had, 'till it ended in his Ruin. I have seen great Abilities rendred utterly useless, by unacountable and unnecessary Delay, and by difficulty of Access, by which a thousand Opportunities are suffered to escape. I have observed the *strongest Shoulders* to sink under too great a load of Business, for want of dividing a due Proportion among others: These and more that might be named, are obvious Failings, which every rational Man may be allowed to discern as well as lament, and wherein the wisest Minister may receive Advice from others of inferior Understanding: But in those Actions where we are not throughly inform'd of all the Motives and Circumstances, 'tis hardly possible, that our Judgment should not be mistaken. I have often been one of the Company, where we have all blamed a Measure taken, which has afterward proved the only one that could possibly have succeeded. Nay I have known those very Men who have formerly been in the Secret of Affairs, when a new Set of People hath come in, offering their Refinements and Conjectures in a very plausible manner upon what was passing, and widely err in all they advanced.

WHATEVER Occasions may have been given for Complaints that *enough hath not been done*, those Complaints should not be carried so far as to make us *forget what hath been done*, which at first was a great deal more than we hoped or thought practicable; and you may be assured, that so much Courage and Address, were not employ'd in the beginning of so great a Work, without a Resolution of carrying it through, as fast as Opportunities would offer. Any of the most sanguine Gentlemen in your Club, would gladly have compounded two Years ago, to have been assured of seeing Affairs in the present Situation: It is principally to the Abilities of *one great Person*, that you, *Gentlemen*, owe the Happiness of meeting together, to cultivate good Principles, and form your selves into a Body for defending your Country against a restless and dangerous Faction. It is to the *Same* we all owe that mighty Change in the most important Posts of the Kingdom; that we see the sacred Person of our *Prince*, encompassed by those whom we ourselves would have chosen, if it had been left to our Power: And if every thing besides, that you could wish, has not been hitherto done, you will be but just to impute it to some powerful though *unknown Impediments*, wherein the Ministry is more to be lamented than blamed: But there is good Reason to hope from the vigorous Proceedings of the Court, that these *Impediments* will in a short time be effectually removed. And one great Motive to hasten the Removal of them, will doubtless be the Reflection upon those dangerous

Consequences which had like to have ensued upon not removing them before. Besides, after so plain and formidable a
Conviction, that mild and moderate Methods meet with no
other Reception or Return, than to serve as Opportunities
to the insatiable Malice of an Enemy; Power will awake to
vindicate it self, and disarm its Opposers, at least, of all *offensive
Weapons*.

CONSIDER, if you please, how hard beset the present
Ministry hath been on every side: By the impossibility of
carrying on the War any longer, without taking the most
desperate Courses; or of recovering *Spain* from the House of
Bourbon, though we could continue it many Years longer:
By the Clamors of a Faction against any Peace without that
Condition, which the most knowing among themselves
allowed to be impracticable: by the secret Cabals of Foreign
Ministers, who have endeavoured to inflame our People, and
Spirited up a sinking Faction to blast all our Endeavours for
Peace, with those Popular Reproaches of *France* and the *Pretender:* Not to mention the Danger they have been in from
private Insinuations of such a Nature, as it was almost impossible
to fence against. These Clouds now begin to blow over,
and those *who are at the Helm*, will have Leisure to look about
them; and compleat what yet remains to be done.

THAT Confederate Body which now makes up the Adverse
Party consists of an Union so monstrous and unnatural, that
in a little time it must of necessity fall to Pieces. The *Dissenters*
with Reason think themselves betray'd and sold by their
Brethren. What they have been told, that the present *Bill*
against *Occasional Conformity*, was to prevent a greater Evil,
is an Excuse too gross to pass; and if any other profound
Refinement were meant, it is now come to nothing. The
remaining Sections of the Party, have no other Tye but that of
an inveterate Hatred and Rancour against those in Power,
without agreeing in any other common Interest; not cemented
by Principle or Personal Friendship, I speak particularly of
their Leaders; and though I know that Court-Enmities are as
inconstant as its Friendships, yet from the difference of
Temper and Principle, as well as the Scars remaining of former

Animosities, I am persuaded their League will not be of long continuance; I know several of them who will never pardon those with whom they are now in Confederacy; and when once they see the present Ministry throughly fixed, they will grow weary of *Hunting upon a cold Scent*, or playing a *desperate Game*, and crumble away.

ON the other side, while the Malice of that Party continues in Vigour; while they yet feel the Bruises of their Fall, which pain them afresh since their late *Disappointment*; they will leave no Arts untried, to recover themselves; and it behoves all who have any regard for the Safety of the Queen or her Kingdom, to join unanimously against an Adversary who will return full fraught with Vengeance upon the first Opportunity that shall offer: and this perhaps is more to be regarded, because that Party seem yet to have a Reserve of Hope, in the *same Quarter from whence their last Reinforcement came*. Neither can any thing cultivate this Hope of theirs so much, as a Disagreement among ourselves, founded upon a Jealousy of the Ministry, who I think need no better a Testimony of their good Intentions, than the incessant *Rage* of the *Party Leaders* against them.

THERE is one Fault which both Sides are apt to charge upon themselves, and very generously commend their Adversaries for the contrary Virtue. The *Tories* acknowledge, that the *Whigs* outdid them in rewarding their Friends, and adhering to each other. The *Whigs* allow the same to the *Tories*. I am apt to think, that the former may a little excell the latter in this Point; for doubtless the *Tories* are less vindicative of the two; and whoever is remiss in *Punishing*, will probably be so in *Rewarding*; tho' at the same time I well remember the Clamors often raised during the Reign of that Party against the Leaders, by those who thought their Merits were not rewarded; and they had Reason on their side; because it is, no doubt, a Misfortune, to forfeit *Honour* and *Conscience* for nothing: But surely the Case is very different at this time, when whoever adheres to the Administration, does Service to God, his Prince, and his Country, as well as contributes to his own private Interest and Safety.

BUT if the *Whig* Leaders were more grateful in rewarding their Friends, it must be avowed likewise, that the Bulk of them was in general more zealous for the Service of their Party, even when abstracted from any private Advantage, as might be observed in a thousand Instances; for which I would likewise commend them, if it were not natural to Mankind to be more *violent in an ill Cause* than a good one.

THE perpetual Discord of Factions, with several Changes of late Years in the very nature of our Government, have controuled many Maxims among us. The *Court* and *Country Party* which used to be the old Division, seems now to be ceased, or suspended for *better Times* and *worse Princes*. The Queen and Ministry are at this time fully in the true Interest of the Kingdom; and therefore the *Court* and *Country* are of a side; and the *Whigs*, who originally were of the latter, are now of neither, but an independent Faction, nursed up by the *Necessities* or *Mistakes* of a late *good, tho' unexperienc'd Prince*. *Court* and *Country* ought therefore to join their Forces against these Common Enemies, till they are entirely dispersed and disabled. It is enough to arm Ourselves against them, when we consider that the greatest Misfortunes which can befall the Nation, are what would most answer their *Interest* and their *Wishes*; a perpetual War encreases their Mony, breaks and beggars their *Landed Enemies*. The Ruin of the Church would please the Dissenters, Deists, and Socinians, whereof the Body of their Party consists. A *Commonwealth*, or a *Protector*, would gratify the *Republican Principles* of some, and the Ambition of others among them.

I WOULD infer from hence, that no Discontents of an inferior nature, such I mean as I have already mentioned, should be carried so far as to give any ill Impression of the present Ministry. If all Things have not been hitherto done as you, *Gentlemen*, could reasonably wish, it can be imputed only to the *secret Instruments* of that Faction. The Truth of this hath appeared from some late Incidents more visible than formerly. Neither do I believe, that any one will now make a Doubt whether a *certain Person* be *in earnest*, after the united and avow'd Endeavours of a whole Party to strike directly at his Head.

WHEN it happens, by some private cross Intrigues, that a great Man has not that Power which is thought due to his Station, he will however probably desire the Reputation of it, without which he neither can preserve the Dignity, nor hardly go through the common Business of his Place; yet is it that Reputation to which he owes all the Envy and Hatred of others, as well as his own Disquiets. Mean time, his expecting Friends impute all their Disappointments to some deep Design, or to his Defect of Good-will, and his Enemies are sure to cry up his Excess of Power; especially in those Points where they are confident it is most shortned. A Minister, in this difficult Case, is sometimes forced to preserve his Credit, by forbearing what *is* in his Power, for fear of discovering how far the Limits extend of what *is not*; or perhaps for fear of shewing an Inclination contrary to that of his Master. Yet all this while he lies under the Reproach of *Delay*, *Unsteddiness*, or *Want of Sincerity*. So that there are many Inconveniences and Dangers, either in discovering or concealing the Want of Power. Neither is it hard to conceive that Ministers may happen to suffer for the *Sins of their Predecessors*, who by their great Abuses and Monopolies of Power and Favour, have taught Princes to be more thrifty for the future in the Distribution of both. And as in common Life, whoever hath been long confined, is very fond of his Liberty, and will not easily endure the very Appearance of Restraint even from those who have been the Instruments of setting him free; so it is with the Recovery of Power; which is usually attended with an undistinguish'd Jealousy, lest it should be *again* invaded. In such a Juncture, I cannot discover why a wise and honest Man should venture to place himself at the Head of Affairs, upon any other Regard than the Safety of his Country, and the Advice of *Socrates*, to *prevent an ill Man from coming in*.

UPON the whole, I do not see any one ground of Suspicion or Dislike, which you, *Gentlemen*, or others who wish well to their Country, may have entertained about Persons or Proceedings, but what may probably be misapprehended even by those who think they have the best Information. Nay, I will venture to go one Step farther, by adding, that although it may not be prudent to speak out upon this Occasion, yet whoever will reason impartially upon the whole State of Affairs, must entirely acquit the Ministry of that Delay and Neutrality which have been laid to their Charge. Or suppose some small part of this Accusation were true, (which I positively know to be otherwise, whereof the World will soon be convinced) yet the Consequences of any Resentment at this time, must either be none at all, or the most fatal that can be imagined; For if the present Ministry be made so uneasy that a Change be thought necessary, Things will return of course into the old Hands of those whose *Little-Fingers will be found heavier than their Predecessors Loins.* The *Whig-Faction* is so dextrous at Corrupting, and the People so susceptible of it, that you cannot be ignorant how easy it will be, after such a Turn of Affairs, upon a new Election, to procure a Majority against you. They will resume their Power with a Spirit like that of *Marius* or *Sylla,* or the last Triumvirate; and those Ministers who have been most censured for too much Hesitation, will fall the first Sacrifices to their Vengeance. But these are the smallest Mischiefs to be apprehended from such returning Exiles. What Security can a Prince hope for his Person or his Crown, or even for the Monarchy itself? He must expect to see his best Friends brought to the Scaffold, for *Asserting his Rights*; to see his *Prerogative* trampled on, and his *Treasures* applied to *feed the Avarice of those who make themselves his Keepers*: To hear himself treated with Insolence and Contempt; to have his *Family purged at Pleasure* by their Humour and Malice; and to retain even the Name and Shadow of a King, no longer than his *Ephori* shall think fit.

THESE are the inevitable Consequences of such a Change of Affairs, as that envenom'd Party is now projecting; which will best be prevented by your firmly adhering to the present Ministry, till this *Domestick Enemy* is out of all possibility of making Head any more.

FINIS.

Some Remarks on the Barrier Treaty

SOME
REMARKS
ON THE
Barrier Treaty,
BETWEEN
HER MAJESTY
AND THE
States - General.

By the AUTHOR of
The Conduct of the ALLIES.

To which are added,

The said BARRIER-TREATY,
with the Two Separate Articles;
Part of the Counter-Project; The
Sentiments of Prince *Eugene* and
Count *Sinzendorf*, upon the said
Treaty; And a Representation of
the *English* Merchants at *Bruges*.

LONDON,
Printed for *John Morphew,* near *Stationers-
Hall,* 1712, Price 6 d.

THE

PREFACE.

WHEN I *Published the Discourse called,* The Conduct of the Allies, *I had Thoughts either of inserting or annexing the* Barrier-Treaty *at length, with such Observations, as I conceived might be useful for publick Information: But that Discourse taking up more room than I designed, after my utmost Endeavours to abbreviate it, I contented my self only with making some few Reflections upon that* famous *Treaty, sufficient, as I thought, to answer the Design of my Book. I have since heard that my Readers in general seemed to wish I had been more particular, and have discovered an Impatience to have that Treaty made publick, especially since it hath been laid before the House of Commons.*

That I may give some Light to the Reader, who is not well vers'd in these Affairs, he may please to know, that a Project for a Treaty of Barrier with the States, *was transmitted hither from* Holland; *but being disapproved of by our Court in several Parts, a new Project, or Scheme of a Treaty, was drawn up here, with many Additions and Alterations. This last was called the* Counter-Project; *and was the Measure whereby the Duke of* Marlborough *and my Lord* Townshend *were Commanded and Instructed to proceed, in Negotiating a* Treaty of Barrier *with the* States. *I have added a Translation of this* Counter-Project, *in those Articles where it differs from the* Barrier-Treaty, *that the Reader, by comparing them together, may judge how punctually those Negotiators observed their Instructions. I have likewise subjoined the Sentiments of Prince* Eugene *of Savoy and the Count* de Sinzendorf, *relating to this Treaty, written (I suppose) while it was negotiating. And lastly, I have added a Copy of the Representation of the* British Merchants *at* Bruges, *signifying what Inconveniencies they already felt, and further apprehended, from this* Barrier-Treaty.

Some Remarks on the Barrier-Treaty.

IMagine a reasonable Person in *China*, were reading the following Treaty, and one who was ignorant of our Affairs, or our Geography; He would conceive their High Mightinesses the States-General, to be some vast powerful Commonwealth, like that of *Rome*, and Her Majesty to be a Petty Prince, like one of those to whom that Republick would sometimes send a *Diadem* for a Present, when they behaved themselves well; otherwise could depose at pleasure, and place whom they thought fit in their stead. Such a Man would think, that the States had taken our Prince and Us into their *Protection*; and in return honoured us so far, as to make use of our Troops as some small Assistance in their Conquests, and the enlargement of their Empire, or to prevent the Incursions of *Barbarians* upon some of their out-lying Provinces. But how must it sound in an *European* Ear, that *Great Britain*, after maintaining a War for so many Years, with so much Glory and Success, and such prodigious Expence; After saving the Empire, *Holland*, and *Portugal*, and almost recovering *Spain*, should, towards the close of a War, enter into a Treaty with Seven *Dutch* Provinces, to secure to them a Dominion larger than their own, which She had conquered for them; to undertake for a great deal more, without stipulating the least Advantage for Her self; and accept as an Equivalent, the mean Condition of those *States* assisting to preserve her Queen on the Throne, whom, by God's Assistance, she is able to defend against all Her Majesty's *Enemies* and *Allies* put together?

SUCH a wild Bargain could never have been made for Us, if the *States* had not found it their Interest to use very *powerful Motives* to the chief Advisers, (I say nothing of the Person immediately employ'd); and if a Party here at Home had not been resolved, for Ends and Purposes very well known, to continue the War as long as they had any occasion for it.

THE *Counter-Project* of this Treaty, made here at *London*, was bad enough in all Conscience: I have said something of it in the *Preface:* Her Majesty's Ministers were instructed to proceed by it in their Negotiation. There was one Point in that Project which would have been of Consequence to *Britain*, and one or two more, where the Advantages of the *States* were not so very exorbitant, and where some Care was taken of the House of *Austria*. Is it possible that *our good Allies and Friends* could not be brought to any Terms with us, unless by striking out every Particular that might do Us any good, and adding still more to Them, where so much was already granted? For instance, the Article about demolishing of *Dunkirk*, surely might have remained, which was of some Benefit to the *States,* as well as of mighty Advantage to Us, and which the *French* King has lately yielded in one of his Preliminaries, tho' clogged with the Demand of an Equivalent, which will owe its difficulty only to this Treaty.

BUT let me now consider the Treaty it self: Among the one and twenty Articles of which it consists, only two have any relation to Us, importing that the *Dutch* are to be Guarantees of our Succession, and are not to enter into any Treaty till the Queen is acknowledged by *France*. We know very well, that it is in Consequence the Interest of the *States*, as much as ours, that *Britain* should be governed by a Protestant Prince. Besides, what is there more in this Guarantee, than in all common Leagues Offensive and Defensive between two Powers, where each is obliged to defend the other against any Invader with all their Strength? Such was the Grand Alliance between the Emperor, *Britain* and *Holland*, which was, or ought to have been, as good a Guarantee of our Succession, to all Intents and Purposes, as this in the *Barrier-Treaty*; and the mutual Engagements in such Alliances have been always reckoned sufficient, without any separate Benefit to either Party.

IT is, no doubt, for the Interest of *Britain*, that the *States* should have a sufficient Barrier against *France:* But their High Mightinesses, for some few Years past, have put a different Meaning upon the word *Barrier*, from what it formerly used to bear, when applied to Them. When the late King was Prince of *Orange*, and commanded their Armies against *France*, it was never once imagined that any of the Towns taken, should belong to the *Dutch*; they were all immediately delivered up to their lawful Monarch; and *Flanders* was only a Barrier to *Holland*, as it was in the Hands of *Spain* rather than *France*. So in the Grand Alliance of 1701, the several Powers promising to endeavour to recover *Flanders* for a Barrier, was understood to be the recovering those Provinces to the King of *Spain*: But in this Treaty, the Style is wholly changed: Here are about twenty Towns and Forts of great Importance, with their Chatellanies and Dependencies (which Dependencies are likewise to be enlarged as much as possible) and the whole Revenues of them, to be under the perpetual Military Government of the *Dutch*, by which that Republick will be entirely Masters of the richest Part of all *Flanders*. And upon any Appearance of War, they may put their Garrisons into any other Place of the *Low-Countries*; and further, the King of *Spain* is to give them a Revenue of four hundred thousand Crowns a Year, to enable them to maintain those Garrisons.

WHY should we wonder, that the *Dutch* are inclined to perpetuate the War, when, by an Article in this Treaty, the King of *Spain* is *not to possess one single Town in the* Low-Countries, *till a Peace is made*. The Duke of *Anjou* at the beginning of this War, maintained six and thirty Thousand Men out of those *Spanish* Provinces he then possessed; To which if we add the many Towns since taken, which were not in the late King of *Spain*'s Possession at the Time of his Death, with all their Territories and Dependencies, it is visible what Forces the *States* may be able to keep, even without any Charge to their peculiar Dominions.

THE Towns and Chatellanies of this Barrier always maintained their Garrisons when they were in the Hands of *France*, and, as it is reported, returned a considerable Sum of Mony into the King's Coffers; yet the King of *Spain* is obliged by this Treaty (as we have already observed) to add, over and above, a Revenue of Four hundred thousand Crowns a Year. We know likewise, that a great part of the Revenue of the *Spanish Netherlands* is already pawned to the *States*; so that after a Peace, nothing will be left to the Sovereign, nor will the People be much eased of the Taxes they at present labour under.

THUS the *States*, by vertue of this *Barrier-Treaty*, will, in effect, be absolute Sovereigns of all *Flanders*, and of the whole Revenues in the utmost Extent.

AND here I cannot, without some Contempt, take notice of a sort of Reasoning offered by several People, that the many Towns we have taken for the *Dutch* are of no Advantage, because the whole Revenues of those Towns are spent in maintaining them. For First, The Fact is manifestly false, particularly as to *Lisle* and some others: Secondly, The *States*, after a Peace, are to have Four hundred thousand Crowns a Year out of the remainder of *Flanders*, which is then to be left to *Spain:* And lastly, Suppose all these acquired Dominions will not bring a Penny into their Treasury; What can be of greater Consequence, than to be able to maintain a mighty Army out of their new Conquests, which before they always did by taxing their natural Subjects?

HOW shall we be able to answer it to King *Charles* the Third, that while we pretend to endeavour restoring him to the entire Monarchy of *Spain*, we join at the same time with the *Dutch* to deprive him of his natural Right to the *Low-Countries?*

BUT suppose by a *Dutch Barrier* must now be understood only what is to be in Possession of the *States*; yet even under this Acceptation of the Word, nothing was originally meant except a *Barrier* against *France*; whereas several Towns demanded by the *Dutch* in this Treaty, can be of no use at all in such a *Barrier*. And this is the Sentiment even of Prince *Eugene* himself (the present Oracle and Idol of the Party here) who says, *That* Dendermond, Ostend, *and the Castle of* Gand, *do in no sort belong to the Barrier, nor can be of other use than to make the States-General Masters of the Low-Countries, and hinder their Trade with* England. And further, *That those who are acquainted with the Country know very well, that* Lier, *and* Hale *to* fortifie, *can give no Security to the* States *as a Barrier, but only raise a Jealousie in the People, that these Places are only fortified in order to block up* Brussels, *and the other great Towns of* Brabant.

In those Towns of *Flanders* where the *Dutch* are to have Garrisons, but the Ecclesiastical and Civil Power to remain to the King of *Spain* after a Peace; the *States* have Power to send Arms, Ammunition and Victuals without paying Customs; under which Pretence they will engross the whole Trade of those Towns, exclusive to all other Nations. This, Prince *Eugene* likewise foresaw, and, in his Observations upon this Treaty here annexed, proposed a Remedy for it.

And if the *Dutch* shall please to think, that the whole *Spanish Netherlands* are not a sufficient Barrier for them, I know no Remedy from the Words of this Treaty, but that we must still go on, and Conquer for them as long as they please. For the Queen is obliged, whenever a Peace is treated, to procure for them *whatever shall be thought necessary* besides; and where their *Necessity* will terminate, is not very easie to foresee.

Could any of Her Majesty's Subjects conceive, that in the Towns we have taken for the *Dutch*, and given into their Possession as a Barrier, either the *States* should demand, or our Ministers allow, that the Subjects of *Britain* should, in respect to their Trade, be used worse in those very Towns, than they were under the late King of *Spain?* Yet this is the Fact, as monstrous as it appears: All Goods going to, or coming from *Newport* or *Ostend*, are to pay the same Duties as those that pass by the *Scheld* under the *Dutch* Forts; And this, in effect, is to shut out all other Nations from Trading to *Flanders*. The *English* Merchants at *Bruges* complain, That *after they have paid the King of* Spain's *Duty for Goods imported at* Ostend, *the same Goods are made liable to further Duties, when they are carried from thence into the Towns of the* Dutch *new Conquests*; and desire only *the same Privileges of Trade they had before the Death of the late King of* Spain, Charles *II.* And in consequence of this Treaty, the *Dutch* have already taken off 8 *per Cent.* from all Goods they send to the *Spanish Flanders*, but left it still upon Us.

But what is very surprising; in the very same Article where *our good Friends and Allies* are wholly shutting us out from Trading in those Towns we have Conquered for them

with so much Blood and Treasure, the Queen is obliged to
procure that the *States* shall be used as favourably in their
Trade over all the King of *Spain*'s Dominions, as Her own
Subjects, or *as the People most favoured*. This I humbly conceive
to be perfect Boys Play, *Cross I win*, and *Pile you lose*; or, *What's
yours is mine*, and *What's mine is my own*. Now if it should
happen that in a Treaty of Peace, some Ports or Towns
should be yielded us for the Security of our Trade in any Part
of the *Spanish* Dominions, at how great a distance soever;
I suppose the *Dutch* would go on with their Boys Play, and
challenge Half by Virtue of that Article: Or would they be
content with the Military Government and the Revenues, and
reckon them among *what shall be thought necessary* for their
Barrier?

THIS prodigious Article is introduced as subsequent to
the Treaty of *Munster*, made about the Year 1648, at a time
when *England* was in the utmost Confusion, and very much to
our Disadvantage. Those Parts in that Treaty, so unjust in
themselves, and so prejudicial to our Trade, ought in reason
to have been remitted, rather than confirmed upon us for the
Time to come: But this is *Dutch* Partnership, to share in all
our beneficial Bargains, and exclude us wholly from theirs,
even from those which we have got for them.

IN one Part of *The Conduct of the Allies*, &c. among other
Remarks upon this Treaty, I make it a Question, whether it
were right in point of Policy or Prudence to call in a Foreign
Power to be Guarantee to our Succession; because by that
means *we put it out of the Power of our own Legislature to alter the
Succession, how much soever the Necessity of the Kingdom may require
it?* To comply with the Cautions of some People, I explained
my Meaning in the following Editions. I was assured that my
Lord Chief Justice affirmed that Passage was Treason; one
of my Answerers, I think, decides as favourably; and I am told,
that Paragraph was read very lately during a Debate, with a
Comment in very injurious Terms, which, perhaps, might
have been spared. That the Legislature should have Power to
change the Succession, whenever the Necessities of the
Kingdom require, is so very useful towards preserving our

Religion and Liberty, that I know not how to recant. The worst of this Opinion is, that at first sight it appears to be *Whiggish*; but the Distinction is thus, The *Whigs* are for changing the Succession when they think fit, though the entire Legislature do not consent; I think it ought never to be done but upon great Necessity, and that with the Sanction of the whole Legislature. Do these Gentlemen of *Revolution-Principles* think it impossible that we should ever have occasion *again* to change our Succession? And if such an Accident should fall out, must we have no Remedy, 'till the Seven Provinces will give their Consent? Suppose that this Virulent Party among us were as able, as some are willing, to raise a *Rebellion* for reinstating them in Power, and would apply themselves to the *Dutch*, as Guarantees of our Succession, to assist them with all their Force, under pretence that the Queen and Ministry, a great Majority of both Houses, and the Bulk of the People were for bringing over *France*, *Popery*, and the *Pretender?* Their High-Mightinesses would, as I take it, be sole Judges of the Controversie, and probably decide it so well, that in some time we might have the Happiness of becoming a Province to *Holland.* I am humbly of Opinion, that there are two Qualities necessary to a Reader, before his Judgment should be allowed; these are, *common Honesty*, and *common Sense*; and that no Man could have misrepresented that Paragraph in my Discourse, unless he were utterly destitute of one or both.

THE Presumptive Successor, and her immediate Heirs, have so established a Reputation in the World, for their Piety, Wisdom, and Humanity, that no Necessity of this kind, is like to appear in their Days; but I must still insist, that it is a diminution to the Independency of the Imperial Crown of *Great Britain*, to call at every Door for Help to put our Laws in execution: And we ought to consider, that if in Ages to come, such a Prince should happen to be in Succession to our Throne, who should be entirely unable to Govern; That very Motive might encline our Guarantees to support him, the more effectually to bring the Rivals of their Trade into Confusion and Disorder.

BUT to return: The Queen is here put under the unreasonable Obligation of being Guarantee of the whole *Barrier-Treaty*, of the *Dutch* having Possession of the said Barrier and the Revenues thereof, before a Peace; of the Payment of Four hundred thousand Crowns by the King of *Spain*; that the *States* shall possess their Barrier even before King *Charles* is in Possession of the *Spanish Netherlands:* Although by the Fifth Article of the Grand Alliance, Her Majesty is under no Obligation to do any thing of this Nature, *except in a General Treaty*.

ALL Kings, Princes, and States are invited to enter into this Treaty, and to be Guarantees of its Execution. This Article, though very frequent in Treaties, seems to look very odly in that of the Barrier: *Popish Princes* are here invited among others, to become Guarantees of our *Protestant Succession:* Every Petty Prince in *Germany* must be intreated to preserve the Queen of *Great Britain* upon Her Throne: The King of *Spain* is invited particularly and by Name, to become Guarantee of the Execution of a Treaty, by which his Allies, who pretend to fight his Battles, and recover his Dominions, strip him in effect of all his Ten Provinces: A clear Reason why they never sent any Forces to *Spain*, and why the Obligation not to enter into a Treaty of Peace with *France*, 'till that entire Monarchy were yielded as a Preliminary, was struck out of the *Counter-Project* by the *Dutch*. They fought only in *Flanders*, because there they only fought for themselves. King *Charles* must needs accept this Invitation very kindly, and stand by with great Satisfaction, while the *Belgick* Lion divides the Prey, and assigns it all to himself. I remember there was a parcel of Soldiers who robbed a Farmer of his Poultry, and then made him wait at Table while they devoured his Victuals, without giving him a Morsel; and upon his Expostulating, had only for Answer, *Why, Sirrah, are not we come here to protect you?* And thus much for this generous Invitation to all Kings and Princes, to lend their Assistance, and become Guarantees, out of pure good Nature, for securing *Flanders* to the *Dutch*.

IN the Treaty of *Ryswick*, no care was taken to oblige the *French* King to acknowledge the Right of Succession in Her present Majesty; for want of which Point being then settled,

France refused to Acknowledge Her for Queen of *Great Britain*, after the late King's Death. This unaccountable Neglect (if it were a Neglect) is here called an *Omission*, and Care is taken to supply it in the next General Treaty of Peace. I mention this occasionally, because I have some subborn Doubts within me, whether it were a *wilful Omission* or no. Neither do I herein reflect in the least upon the Memory of His late Majesty, whom I entirely acquit of any Imputation upon this Matter. But when I recollect the Behaviour, the Language, and the Principles of *some certain Persons* in those Days, and compare them with that *Omission*; I am tempted to draw some Conclusions, which a certain Party would be more ready to call False and Malicious, than to prove them so.

I MUST here take leave (because it will not otherwise fall in my way) to say a few Words in return to a Gentleman, I know not of what Character or Calling, who has done me the Honour to write Three Discourses against that Treatise of the *Conduct of the Allies*, &c. and promises, for my Comfort, to conclude all in a Fourth. I pity Answerers with all my Heart, for the many Disadvantages they lie under. My Book did a World of Mischief (as he calls it) before his First Part could possibly come out; and so went on through the Kingdom, while his limped slowly after, and if it arrived at all, it was too late; for Peoples Opinions were already fixed. His manner of answering me is thus: Of those Facts which he pretends to examine, some he resolutely denies, others he endeavours to extenuate, and the rest he distorts with such unnatural Turns, that I would engage, by the same Method, to disprove any History, either Ancient or Modern. Then the whole is Interlarded with a thousand injurious Epithets and Appellations, which heavy Writers are forced to make use of, as a supply for that want of Spirit and Genius they are not born to: Yet, after all, he allows a very great Point for which I contend, confessing in plain Words, that the Burthen of the War has chiefly lain upon Us; and thinks it sufficient for the *Dutch*, that, next to *England*, they have born the greatest Share. And is not this the great Grievance of which the whole Kingdom complains? I am inclined to think that my Intelli-

gence was at least as good as his; and some of it, I can assure
him, came from Persons of his own Party, though perhaps
not altogether so inflamed. Hitherto therefore, the Matter is
pretty equal, and the World may believe Him or Me, as they
please. But, I think, the great Point of Controversie between
us, is, whether the Effects and Consequences of Things follow
better from His Premises or mine: And there I will not be
satisfied, unless he will allow the whole Advantage to be on
my side. Here is a flourishing Kingdom brought to the Brink
of Ruin, by a *most Successful and Glorious War of* Ten Years,
under an *Able, Diligent, Loyal Ministry*; a *most Faithful, Just,
and Generous Commander*; and in Conjunction with the most
Hearty, Reasonable, and Sincere Allies: This is the Case, as
that Author represents it. I have heard a Story, I think it
was of the Duke of ——— who playing at Hazard at the
Groom-Porters in much Company, held in a great many
Hands together, and drew a huge Heap of Gold; but, in the
heat of Play, never observed a Sharper, who came once or
twice under his Arm, and swept a great deal of it into his
Hat: The Company thought it had been one of his *Servants:*
When the Duke's Hand was out, they were talking how much
he had won: Yes, said he, I held in very long; yet, methinks,
I have won but very little: They told him, his SERVANT had
got the rest in his Hat; and then he found he was cheated.

IT hath been my good Fortune to see the most important
Facts that I have advanced, justify'd by the Publick Voice;
which let this Author do what he can, will incline the World to
believe, that I may be right in the rest: And I solemnly declare,
that I have not wilfully committed the least Mistake. I stopt
the Second Edition, and made all possible Enquiries among
those who I thought could best inform me, in order to correct
any Error I could hear of: I did the same to the Third and
Fourth Editions, and then left the Printer to his liberty. This I
take for a more effectual Answer to all Cavils, than an hundred
Pages of Controversy.

BUT what disgusts me from having any thing to do with
this Race of *Answer-jobbers*, is, that they have no sort of Conscience in their Dealings: To give one Instance in this

Gentleman's Third Part, which I have been lately looking into. When I talk of the *most Petty Princes*, he says, I mean *Crowned Heads:* When I say, *the Soldiers of those Petty Princes are ready to rob or starve at Home:* He says I call *Kings* and *Crowned Heads, Robbers* and *Highwaymen.* This is what the *Whigs* call answering a Book.

I CANNOT omit one Particular, concerning this Author, who is so positive in asserting his own Facts, and contradicting mine: He affirms, *That the Business of* Thoulon *was discovered by the Clerk of a certain Great Man, who was then Secretary of State.* It is neither wise, nor for the Credit of his Party, to put us in mind either of *that Secretary,* or of *that Clerk*; however, so it happens, that nothing relating to the Affair of *Thoulon* did ever pass through that Secretary's Office: Which I here affirm, with great Phlegm, leaving the Epithets of *False, Scandalous, Villainous,* and the rest, to the Author and his Fellows.

BUT to leave this Author; let us consider the Consequence of our Triumphs, upon which some set so great a Value, as to think that nothing less than the Crown can be a sufficient Reward for the Merit of the General: We have not enlarged our Dominions by one Foot of Land: Our Trade, which made us considerable in the World, is either given up by Treaties, or clogged with Duties, which interrupt and daily lessen it: We see the whole Nation groaning under excessive Taxes of all sorts, to raise three Millions of Money for payment of the Interest of those Debts we have contracted. Let us look upon the reverse of the Medal, we shall see our Neighbours, who in their utmost Distress, called for our Assistance, become, by this Treaty, even in time of Peace, Masters of a more considerable Country than their own; in a condition to strike Terror into Us, with fifty thousand *Veterans* ready to invade us, from that Country which we have conquered for them; and to commit insolent Hostilities upon us, in all other Parts, as they have lately done in the *East-Indies.*

The *Barrier-Treaty* between Her Majesty and the
States-General.

HER *Majesty, the Queen of* Great Britain, *and the Lords
the States-General of the United Provinces, having considered
how much it concerns the Quiet and the Security of their
Kingdoms and States, and the publick Tranquility, to maintain and
to secure on one side the Succession to the Crown of* Great Britain,
*in such manner as it is now established by the Laws of the Kingdom;
and on the other side, That the said States-General of the* United
Provinces *should have a strong and sufficient Barrier against* France,
*and others, who would surprise or attack them: And Her Majesty
and the said States-General apprehending, with just reason, the
Troubles and the Mischiefs which may happen, in relation to this
Succession, if at any time there should be any Person or any Power
who should call it in Question; and, That the Countries and States of
the said Lords the States-General, were not furnished with such a
Barrier. For these said Reasons, Her said Majesty the Queen of*
Great Britain, *tho' in the vigour of Her Age, and enjoying perfect
Health, (which may God preserve Her in many Years) out of an
effect of Her usual Prudence and Piety, has thought fit to enter, with
the Lords the States-General of the* United Provinces, *into a particular Alliance and Confederacy, the principal End and only Aim
of which, shall be the publick Quiet and Tranquility; and to prevent,
by Measures taken in time, all the Events which might one day
excite new Wars. It is with this View that Her* British *Majesty
has given Her full Power to agree upon some Articles of a Treaty,
in addition to the Treaties and Alliances that She has already with
the Lords the States-General of the* United Provinces, *to Her
Ambassador Extraordinary and Plenipotentiary,* Charles *Viscount*
Townshend, *Baron of* Lyn-Regis, *Privy-Councellor of Her* British
*Majesty, Captain of Her said Majesty's Yeomen of the Guard,
and Her Lieutenant in the County of* Norfolk: *And the Lords the
States-General of the* United Provinces, *the* Sieurs John de
Welderen, *Lord of* Valburgh, *Great Bayliff of the* Lower Betuwe,
of the Body of the Nobility of the Province of Guelder; Frederick
Baron of Reede, *Lord of* Lier, *St.* Anthony *and* T'er Lee, *of the*

Order of the Nobility of the Province of Holland *and* West Frize-
land; Anthony Heinsius, *Counsellor Pensionary of the Province of*
Holland *and* West-Frizeland, *Keeper of the Great Seal, and Super-
Intendant of the Fiefs of the same Province*; Cornelius Van Gheel,
Lord of Spanbroek Bulkesteyn, *&c.* Gedeon Hoeuft, *Canon of
the Chapter of the Church of St.* Peter *at* Utrecht, *and elected
Counsellor in the States of the Province of* Utrecht; Hessel van
Sminia, *Secretary of the Chamber of Accounts of the Province of*
Frizeland; Ernest Ittersum, *Lord of* Osterhof, *of the Body of the
Nobility of the Province of* Overyssel; *and* Wicher Wichers, *Senator
of the City of* Groningen; *all Deputies to the Assembly of the said
Lords the States-General on the part, respectively, of the Provinces
of* Guelder, Holland, West-Friezeland, Zeeland, Utrecht, Frize-
land, Overyssell, *and* Groninguen, *and* Ommelands, *who, by
Vertue of their full Powers, are agreed upon the following Articles.*

Article I.

THE Treaties of Peace, Friendship, Alliance and Confederacy between Her *Britannick Majesty* and the *States-
General* of the *United Provinces*, shall be approved and
confirmed by the present Treaty, and shall remain in their
former Force and Vigour, as if they were inserted Word for
Word.

II.

THE Succession to the Crown of *England* having been
Setled by an Act of Parliament passed the Twelfth Year of
the Reign of His late Majesty King *William* the Third; the
Title of which is, *An Act for the further Limitation of the Crown,
and better Securing the Rights and Liberties of the Subject:* And
lately, in the Sixth Year of the Reign of Her present Majesty,
this Succession having been again Established and Confirmed
by another Act made for the *greater Security of Her Majesty's
Person and Government, and the Succession to the Crown of* Great
Britain, &c. *in the Line of the most Serene House of* Hanover,
and in the Person of the Princess Sophia, *and of Her Heirs,
Successors and Descendants, Male and Female, already Born or to*

be Born: And though no Power has any Right to Oppose the Laws made upon this Subject, by the Crown and Parliament of *Great Britain,* if it should happen, nevertheless, that under any Pretence, or by any Cause whatever, any Person, or any Power or State may pretend to dispute the Establishment which the Parliament has made of the aforesaid Succession, in the most Serene House of *Hanover,* to Oppose the said Succession, to Assist or Favour those who may Oppose it, whether directly or indirectly, by open War, or by fomenting Seditions and Conspiracies against Her or Him to whom the Crown of *Great Britain* shall descend, according to the Acts aforesaid; The *States-General* engage and promise to Assist and Maintain, in the said Succession, Her or Him to whom it shall belong, by Vertue of the said Acts of Parliament, to assist them in taking Possession, if they should not be in actual Possession, and to Oppose those who would disturb them in the taking such Possession, or in the actual Possession of the aforesaid Succession.

III.

HER said Majesty and the *States-General,* in Consequence of the Fifth Article of the Alliance concluded between the Emperor, the late King of *Great Britain,* and the *States-General,* the 7th of *September,* 1701, will employ all their Force to recover the rest of the *Spanish Low-Countries.*

IV.

AND further, they will endeavour to Conquer as many Towns and Forts as they can, in order to their being a Barrier and Security to the said *States.*

V.

AND whereas, according to the Ninth Article of the said Alliance, it is to be agreed, amongst other Matters, how and in what manner the *States* shall be made Safe by means of this Barrier, the Queen of *Great Britain* will use Her Endeavours to procure, that in the Treaty of Peace it may be agreed, that all

the *Spanish Low-Countries*, and what else may be found necessary, whether Conquered or Unconquered Places, shall serve
as a Barrier to the *States*.

VI.

THAT to this end their High Mightinesses shall have the
Liberty to put and keep Garrison, to change, augment and
diminish it as they shall judge proper, in the Places following:
Namely, *Newport, Furnes*, with the Fort of *Knocke, Ipres, Menin*,
the Town and Cittadel of *Lisle, Tournay* and its Cittadel, *Condé,
Valenciennes*; and the Places which shall from henceforward be
Conquered from *France. Maubeuge, Charleroy, Namur* and its
Cittadel, *Liere, Hale* to Fortifie, the Ports of *Perle, Philippe,
Damme*, the Castle of *Gand*, and *Dendermonde*; the Fort of St.
Donas being joined to the Fortifications of the Sluice, and
being entirely incorporated with it, shall remain and be
yielded in Property to the *States*. The Fort of *Rodenhuysen*,
on this side *Gand*, shall be Demolished.

VII.

THE said *States-General* may, in case of an apparent Attack,
or War, put as many Troops as they shall think necessary
in all the Towns, Places and Forts in the *Spanish Low-Countries*,
where the Reason of War shall require it.

VIII.

THEY may likewise send into the Towns, Forts and Places,
where they shall have their Garrisons, without any Hindrance,
and without paying any Duties, Provisions, Ammunitions of
War, Arms and Artillery, Materials for the Fortifications,
and all that shall be found convenient and necessary for the said
Garrisons and Fortifications.

IX.

THE said *States-General* shall also have Liberty to Appoint
in the Towns, Forts and Places of their Barrier, mentioned in
the foregoing Sixth Article, where they may have Garrisons,

I

such Governors and Commanders, Majors and other Officers, as they shall find proper, who shall not be subject to any other Orders, whatsoever they may be, or from whence soever they may come, relating to the Security and Military Government of the said Places, but only to those of their High Mightinesses (exclusively of all others); still preserving the Rights and Privileges, as well Ecclesiastical as Political, of King *Charles* the Third.

X.

THAT, besides, the said *States* shall have Liberty to Fortifie the said Towns, Places and Forts which belong to them, and Repair the Fortifications of them, in such manner as they shall judge necessary; and further to do whatever shall be useful for their Defence.

XI.

IT is agreed, That the *States-General* shall have all the Revenues of the Towns, Places, Jurisdictions, and their Dependencies, which they shall have for their Barrier from *France*, which were not in the Possession of the Crown of *Spain*, at the time of the Death of the late King *Charles* the Second; and besides, a Million of Livres shall be settled for the Payment of One hundred thousand Crowns every three Months, out of the clearest Revenues of the *Spanish Low-Countries*, which the said King was then in Possession of; both which are for maintaining the Garrisons of the *States*, and for supplying the Fortifications, as also the Magazines, and other necessary Expences, in the Towns and Places above-mentioned. And that the said Revenues may be sufficient to support these Expences, Endeavours shall be used for enlarging the Dependencies and Jurisdictions aforesaid, as much as possible; and particularly for including with the Jurisdiction of *Ipres*, that of *Cassel*, and the Forest of *Niepe*; and with the Jurisdiction of *Lisle*, the Jurisdiction of *Douay*, both having been so joined before the present War.

XII.

THAT no Town, Fort, Place, or Country of the *Spanish Low-Countries*, shall be granted, transferred, or given, or descend to the Crown of *France*, or any one of the Line of *France*, neither by vertue of any Gift, Sale, Exchange, Marriage, Agreement, Inheritance, Succession by Will, or through want of Will, from no Title whatsoever, nor in any other manner whatever, nor be put into the Power or under the Authority of the most Christian King, or any one of the Line of *France*.

XIII.

AND whereas the said *States-General*, in Consequence of the Ninth Article of the said Alliance, are to make a Convention or Treaty with King *Charles* the Third, for putting the *States* in a Condition of Safety, by means of the said Barrier, the Queen of *Great Britain* will do what depends upon Her, that all the foregoing Particulars, relating to the Barrier of the *States*, may be inserted in the aforesaid Treaty or Convention; and that Her said Majesty will continue Her good Offices, 'till the above-mentioned Convention, between the *States* and the said King *Charles* the Third, be concluded, agreeably to what is before-mentioned; and that Her Majesty will be Guarantee of the said Treaty or Convention.

XIV.

AND that the said *States* may enjoy from henceforward, as much as possible, a Barrier for the *Spanish Low-Countries*, they shall be permitted to put their Garrisons in the Towns already taken, and which may hereafter be so, before the Peace be concluded and ratified. And in the mean time the said King *Charles* the Third shall not be allowed to enter into Possession of the said *Spanish Low-Countries*, neither entirely nor in part; and during that time the Queen shall assist their High Mightinesses to maintain them in the Enjoyment of the Revenues, and to find the Million of Livres a Year above-mentioned.

XV.

AND whereas their High Mightinesses have Stipulated by the Treaty of *Munster*, in the Fourteenth Article, That the River *Schelde*, as also the Canals of *Sas*, *Swyn*, and other Mouths of the Sea bordering thereupon, should be kept shut on the Side of the *States:*

AND in the Fifteenth Article, That the Ships and Commodities going in and coming out of the Harbours of *Flanders*, shall be and remain charged with all such Imposts and other Duties, as are raised upon Commodities going and coming along the *Schelde*, and the other Canals above-mentioned:

THE Queen of *Great Britain* promises and engages, That their High Mightinesses shall never be disturbed in their Right and Possession, in that respect, neither directly nor indirectly; as also that the Commerce shall not, in prejudice of the said Treaty, be made more easy by the Sea-Ports, than by the Rivers, Canals and Mouths of the Sea, on the side of the States of the *United Provinces*, neither directly nor indirectly.

AND whereas by the 16th and 17th Articles of the same Treaty of *Munster*, his Majesty the King of *Spain*, is obliged to treat the Subjects of their High Mightinesses as favourably as the Subjects of *Great Britain* and the *Hans Towns*, who were then the People the most favourably treated; Her *Britanick* Majesty and their High Mightinesses promise likewise, to take care that the Subjects of *Great Britain*, and of their High Mightinesses, shall be treated in the *Spanish Low-Countries*, as well as in all *Spain*, the Kingdoms and States belonging to it, equally, and as well the one as the other, as favourably as the People the most favoured.

XVI.

THE said Queen and States-General oblige themselves to furnish, by Sea and Land, the Succours and Assistance necessary to maintain, by force, Her said Majesty in the quiet possession of Her Kingdoms; and the most Serene House of *Hanover* in the said Succession, in the manner it is settled by the Acts of Parliament before-mentioned; and to maintain the said States-General in the possession of the said Barrier.

XVII.

AFTER the Ratifications of this Treaty, a particular Convention shall be made of the Conditions by which the said Queen, and the said Lords, the States-General, will engage themselves to furnish the Succours which shall be thought necessary, as well by Sea as by Land.

XVIII.

IF Her *British* Majesty, or the States-General of the *United Provinces*, be attacked by any Body whatsoever, by reason of this Convention, they shall mutually assist one another with all their Forces, and become Guarantees of the Execution of the said Convention.

XIX.

THERE shall be invited and admitted into the present Treaty, as soon as possible, all the Kings, Princes and States, who shall be willing to enter into the same, particularly his Imperial Majesty, the Kings of *Spain* and *Prussia*, and the Elector of *Hanover*. And Her *British* Majesty, and the States-General of the *United Provinces*, and each of them in particular, shall be permitted to require and invite those whom they shall think fit to require and invite, to enter into this Treaty, and to be Guarantees of its Execution.

XX.

AND as Time has shewn the Omission which was made in the Treaty signed at *Ryswick* in the Year 1697, between *England* and *France*, in respect of the Right of the Succession of *England*, in the Person of Her Majesty the Queen of *Great Britain* now reigning; and that for want of having settled in that Treaty this indisputable Right of Her Majesty, *France* refused to acknowledge Her for Queen of *Great Britain*, after the Death of the late King *William* the Third, of glorious Memory: Her Majesty, the Queen of *Great Britain*, and the Lords, the

States-General of the *United Provinces*, do agree and engage themselves likewise, not to enter into any Negociation or Treaty of Peace with *France*, before the Title of Her Majesty to the Crown of *Great Britain*, as also the Right of Succession of the most Serene House of *Hanover*, to the aforesaid Crown, in the manner it is settled and established by the before-mentioned Acts of Parliament, be fully acknowledged, as a Preliminary by *France*, and that *France* has promised at the same time to remove out of its Dominions the Person who pretends to be King of *Great Britain*; and that no Negociation nor formal discussion of the Articles of the said Treaty of Peace shall be entered into, but jointly and at the same time with the said Queen, or with Her Ministers.

XXI.

HER *British* Majesty, and the Lords the *States-General* of the *United Provinces*, shall ratify and confirm all that is contained in the present Treaty, within the space of four Weeks, to be reckoned from the Day of the Signing. In Testimony whereof, the underwritten Ambassador Extraordinary and Plenipotentiary of Her *British* Majesty, and the Deputies of the Lords the *States-General* have signed this present Treaty, and have affixed their Seals thereunto.

At the Hague, *the 29th of* October, *in the Year* 1709.

(L. S.) *Townshend.*

(L. S.) *J. V. Welderen.*
(L. S.) *J. B. Van Reede.*
(L. S.) *A. Heinsius.*
(L. S.) *G. Hoeuft.*
(L. S.) *H. Sminia.*
(L. S.) *E. V. Ittersum.*
(L. S.) *W. Wichers.*

The Separate Article.

AS in the Preliminary Articles Signed here at the *Hague* the 28th of *May*, 1709, by the Plenipotentiaries of his Imperial Majesty, of Her Majesty the Queen of *Great Britain*, and of the Lords the States-General of the *United*

Provinces, it is Stipulated, amongst other Things, that the Lords the States-General shall have, with entire Property and Sovereignty, the Upper Quarter of *Guelder*, according to the Fifty-second Article of the Treaty of *Munster* of the Year 1648; as also that the Garrisons which are or hereafter shall be on the Part of the Lords the States-General in the Town of *Huy*, the Cittadel of *Liege*, and in the Town of *Bonne*, shall remain there, 'till it shall be otherwise agreed upon with his Imperial Majesty and the Empire. And as the Barrier which is this Day agreed upon in the principal Treaty, for the mutual Guaranty between Her *British* Majesty and the Lords the States-General, cannot give to the *United Provinces* the Safety for which it is Established, unless it be well secured from one end to the other, and that the Communication of it be well joined together; for which the Upper Quarter of *Guelder*, and the Garrisons in the Cittadel of *Liege*, *Huy* and *Bonne* are absolutely necessary: Experience having thrice shewn, that *France* having a design to attack the *United Provinces*, has made use of the Places above-mentioned in order to come at them, and to penetrate into the said Provinces. That further, in respect to the Equivalent for which the Upper Quarter of *Guelder* is to be yielded to the *United Provinces*, according to the Fifty-second Article of the Treaty of *Munster* above-mentioned, His Majesty King *Charles* the Third will be much more gratified and advantaged in other Places, than that Equivalent can avail. So that to the end the Lords the States-General may have the Upper Quarter of *Guelder*, with entire Property and Sovereignty, and that the said Upper Quarter of *Guelder* may be yielded in this manner to the said Lords the States-General, in the Convention, or the Treaty that they are to make with His Majesty King *Charles* the Third, according to the Thirteenth Article of the Treaty concluded this Day; as also that their Garrisons in the Cittadel of *Liege*, in that of *Huy* and in *Bonne*, may remain there, until it be otherwise agreed upon with his Imperial Majesty and the Empire, Her Majesty, the Queen of *Great Britain*, engages Herself and promises by this separate Article, which shall have the same Force as if it was inserted in the principal Treaty, to make the same Efforts for all this as She has engaged Herself to make, for their obtaining the Barrier in the *Spanish Low-Countries*. In Testimony whereof the Underwritten Ambassador-Extraordinary and Plenipotentiary of Her *British* Majesty, and Deputies of the Lords the States-General, have Signed the present Separate Article, and have affixed their Seals thereunto. *At the* Hague, *the* 29*th of* October, 1709.

(L. S.) *Townshend.*

(L. S.) *J. V. Welderen.*
(L. S.) *J. B. van Reede.*
(L. S.) *A. Heinsius.*
(L. S.) *G. Hoeuft.*
(L. S.) *H. Sminia.*
(L. S.) *E. V. Ittersum.*
(L. S.) *W. Wichers.*

The Second Separate Article.

AS the Lords the States-General have represented, That in *Flanders*, the Limits between *Spanish Flanders*, and that of the *States*, are settled in such a manner, as that the Land belonging to the *States* is extreamly narrow there; so that in some Places the Territory of *Spanish Flanders* extends it self to the Fortifications, and under the Cannon of the Places, Towns, and Forts of the *States*, which occasions many Inconveniencies, as has been seen by an Example a little before the beginning of the present War, when a Fort was designed to have been built under the Cannon of the *Sas van Gand*, under pretence, that it was upon the Territory of *Spain*. And as it is necessary for avoiding these and other sorts of Inconveniencies, that the Land of the *States*, upon the Confines of *Flanders* should be enlarged, and that the Places, Towns and Forts should, by that means, be better covered; Her *British* Majesty entring into the just Motives of the said Lords the States-General in this respect, promises and engages Herself by this *Separate Article*, That in the Convention that the said Lords, the States-General, are to make with His Majesty, King *Charles* the Third, She will so assist them, as that it may be agreed, That by the Cession to the said Lords, the States-General, of the Property of an Extent of Land necessary to obviate such like and other Inconveniencies, their Limits in *Flanders* shall be enlarged more conveniently for their Security, and those of the *Spanish Flanders* removed farther from their Towns, Places and Forts, to the End that these may not be so exposed any more. In Testimony whereof, the underwritten Ambassador Extraordinary and Plenipotentiary of Her *British* Majesty, and Deputies of the Lords the States-General, have Signed the present *Separate Article*, and have affixed their Seals thereunto. *At the* Hague, *the* 29*th of* October, 1709.

(L. S.) *Townshend.*

(L. S.) *J. B. van Reede.*
(L. S.) *A. Heinsius.*
(L. S.) *G. Hoeuft.*
(L. S.) *H. Sminia.*
(L. S.) *E. V. Ittersum.*

The Articles *of the* Counter-Project, *which were struck out or altered by the* Dutch, *in the* Barrier-Treaty: *With some* Remarks.

Article VI.

TO this End, their High Mightinesses shall have Power to put and keep Garrisons in the following Places, *viz*. *Newport, Knock, Menin,* the Cittadel of *Lisle, Tournay, Conde, Valenciennes, Namur* and its Cittadel, *Liere, Hale* to *fortifie,* the Fort of *Perle, Damme,* and the Castle of *Gand.*

REMARKS.

In the Barrier-Treaty, *the* States *added the following Places to those mentioned in this Article,* viz. Furnes, Ipres, *Town of* Lisle, Maubeuge, Charleroy, Philippe, *Fort of* St. Donas (*which is to be in Property to the* States) *and the Fort of* Rodenhuysen, *to be Demolished. To say nothing of the other Places,* Dendermond *is the Key of all* Brabant; *and the Demolishing of the Fort of* Rodenhuysen, *situate between* Gand *and* Sas van Gand, *can only serve to Defraud the King of* Spain *of the Duties upon Goods Imported and Exported there.*

Article VII.

THE said *States* may put into the said Towns, Forts and Places, and in case of open War with *France*, into all the other Towns, Places and Forts, whatever Troops the Reason of War shall require.

REMARKS. *But in the* Barrier-Treaty *it is said*, in case of an apparent Attack or War, *without specifying against* France: *Neither is the Number of Troops limited to what the Reason of War shall require, but what the* States *shall think necessary*.

ARTICLE IX. *Besides some smaller Differences, ends with a* Salvo, *not only for the Ecclesiastical and Civil Rights of the King of* Spain, *but likewise for his Revenues in the said Towns*; *which* Revenues, *in the* Barrier-Treaty, *are all given to the* States.

Article XI.

THE Revenues of the Chattellanies and Dependencies of the Towns and Places, which the *States* shall have for their Barrier against *France*, and which were not in possession of the Crown of *Spain*, at the late King of *Spain*'s Death, shall be settled to be a Fund for maintaining Garrisons, and providing for the Fortifications and Magazines, and other necessary Charges of the said Towns of the Barrier.

REMARKS. *I desire the Reader to compare this with the Eleventh Article of the* Barrier-Treaty, *where he will see how prodigiously it is enlarged*.

Article XIV.

ALL this is to be without Prejudice to such other Treaties and Conventions as the Queen of *Great Britain*, and their High Mightinesses, may think fit to make for the future with the said King *Charles* the Third, relating to the said *Spanish Netherlands*, or to the said *Barrier*.

Article XV.

AND to the End that the said *States* may enjoy, at present, as much as it is possible, a *Barrier* in the *Spanish Netherlands*, they shall be permitted to put their Garrisons in the chief Towns already taken, or that may be taken, before a Peace be made.

REMARKS. *These Two Articles are not in the* Barrier-Treaty, *but Two others in their stead; to which I refer the Reader. And indeed it was highly necessary for the* Dutch *to strike out the former of these Articles, when so great a part of the Treaty is so highly and manifestly prejudicial to* Great Britain, *as well as to the King of* Spain; *especially the Two Articles inserted in the place of these, which I desire the Reader will Examine.*

Article XX.

AND whereas by the 5th and 9th Articles of the Alliance between the Emperor, the late King of *Great Britain*, and the States-General, concluded the 7th of *September* 1701, it is agreed and stipulated, That the Kingdoms of *Naples* and *Sicily*, with all the Dependencies of the Crown of *Spain* in *Italy*, shall be recovered from the Possession of *France*, as being of the last Consequence to the Trade of both Nations, as well as the *Spanish Netherlands*, for a Barrier for the *States-General*; therefore the said Queen of *Great Britain*, and the States-General, agree and oblige themselves, not to enter into any Negociation or Treaty of Peace with *France*, before the Restitution of the said Kingdoms of *Naples* and *Sicily*, with all the Dependencies of the Crown of *Spain* in *Italy*, as well as the *Spanish Low-Countries*, with the other Towns and Places in the Possession of *France*, above-mentioned in this Treaty; and also after the manner specified in this Treaty; as likewise all the rest of the entire Monarchy of *Spain*, be yielded by *France* as a Preliminary.

Article XXII.

AND whereas Experience hath shewn of what Importance it is to *Great Britain* and the *United Provinces*, that the Fortress and Port of *Dunkirk* should not be in the Possession of *France*, in the Condition they are at present; the Subjects of both Nations having undergone such great Losses, and suffered so much in their Trade, by the Prizes taken from them by Privateers set out in that Port; insomuch that *France*, by her unmeasurable Ambition, may be always tempted to make some Enterprizes upon the Territories of the Queen of *Great Britain* and their High Mightinesses, and interrupt the Publick Repose and Tranquility; for the Preservation of which, and the Balance of *Europe* against the exorbitant Power of *France*, the Allies engaged themselves in this long and burthensome War; therefore the said Queen of *Great Britain*, and their High Mightinesses agree and oblige themselves, not to enter into any Negotiation or Treaty of Peace with *France*, before it shall be yielded and stipulated by *France* as a Preliminary, that all the Fortifications of the said Town of *Dunkirk*, and the Forts that depend upon it, be entirely demolished and razed, and that the Port be entirely ruined, and rendred impracticable.

REMARKS. *These two Articles are likewise omitted in the* Barrier-Treaty; *whereof the first regards particularly the Interests of the House of* Austria; *and the other about Demolishing of* Dunkirk, *those of* Great Britain. *It is something strange, that the late Ministry, whose Advocates raise such a Clamour about the Necessity of Recovering* Spain *from the House of* Bourbon, *should suffer the* Dutch *to strike out this Article*; *which, I think, clearly shows, the Reason why the* States *never troubled themselves with the Thoughts of Reducing* Spain, *or even Recovering* Milan, Naples, *and* Sicily, *to the Emperor*; *but were wholly fix'd upon the Conquest of* Flanders, *because they had determined those Provinces as a Property for themselves.*

As for the Article about Demolishing of Dunkirk, *I am not at all surprized to find it struck out*; *the Destruction of that Place, though it would be useful to the* States, *doth more nearly import* Britain, *and was therefore a Point that such Ministers could more easily get over.*

The Sentiments of Prince Eugene *of* Savoy, *and of the Count*
de Sinzendorf, *relating to the* Barrier *of the* States-
General, *to the Upper-Quarter of* Guelder, *and to the*
Towns *of the Electorate of* Cologn, *and of the Bishoprick*
of Liege.

ALtho' the Orders and Instructions of the Courts of
Vienna and *Barcelona,* upon the Matters above-mentioned, do not go so far, as to give Directions for
what follows; notwithstanding, the Prince and Count above-
mentioned, considering the present State of Affairs, are of the
following Opinion:

First, That the Counter-Project of *England,* relating to the
Places where the States-General may put and keep Garrisons,
ought to be followed, except *Lier, Halle to fortify,* and the
Castle of *Gand:* Provided likewise, that the Sentiments of
England be particularly conformed to, relating to *Dendermond*
and *Ostend,* as Places in no wise belonging to the Barrier;
and which, as well as the Castle of *Gand,* can only serve to
make the States-General Masters of the *Low-Countries,* and
hinder Trade with *England.* And as to *Lier* and *Halle,* those
who are acquainted with the Country, know, that these Towns
cannot give any Security to the States-General, but can only
make People believe that these Places being fortified, would
rather serve to block up *Brussels,* and the other great Cities of
Brabant.

Secondly, As to what is said in the Seventh Article of the
Counter-Project of *England,* relating to the Augmentation of
Garrisons, in the Towns of the Barrier, in case of an open War;
this is agreeable to the Opinions of the said Prince and Count;
who think likewise, that there ought to be added to the Eighth
Article, That no Goods or Merchandise should be sent into
the Towns where the States-General shall have Garrisons,
nor be comprehended under the Names of *such Things, as the*
said Garrisons and Fortifications shall have need of: And that to
this End, the said Things shall be inspected in those Places

where they are to pass; as likewise, the Quantity shall be settled that the Garrisons may want.

Thirdly, As to the Ninth Article, relating to the Governours and Commanders of those Towns, Forts and Places, where the States-General shall have their Garrisons, the said *Prince* and *Count* are of Opinion, That the said Governours and Commanders ought to take an Oath, as well to the King of *Spain*, as to the States-General: But they may take a particular Oath to the Latter, That they will not admit Foreign Troops without their Consent, and that they will depend exclusively upon the said States, in whatever regards the Military Power. But at the same time they ought exclusively to promise the King of *Spain*, That they will not intermeddle in the Affairs of Law, Civil Power, Revenues, or any other Matters, Ecclesiastical or Civil, unless at the desire of the King's Officers, to assist them in the Execution: In which case the said Commanders should be obliged not to refuse them.

Fourthly, As to the Tenth Article, there is nothing to be added, unless that the States-General, may repair and encrease the Fortifications of the Towns, Places and Forts, where they shall have their Garrisons; but this at their own Expence. Otherwise, under that Pretext, they might seize all the Revenues of the Country.

Fifthly, As to the Eleventh Article, they think the States ought not to have the Revenues of the Chattellanies and Dependencies of these Towns and Places which are to be their Barrier against *France*; this being a sort of Sovereignty, and very prejudicial to the Ecclesiastical and Civil Oeconomy of the Country. But the said Prince and Count are of Opinion, That the States-General ought to have, for the Maintenance of their Garrisons and Fortifications, a Sum of Money of a Million and half, or two Millions of Florins, which they ought to receive from the King's Officers, who shall be ordered to pay that Sum, before any other Payment.

Sixthly, And the Convention which shall be made, on this Affair, between his Catholick Majesty and the States-General, shall be for a limited Time.

THESE are the utmost Conditions to which the said Prince

and Count think it possible for his Catholick Majesty to be brought; and they declare at the same time, that their Imperial and Catholick Majesties will sooner abandon the *Low-Countries,* than take them upon other Conditions, which would be equally Expensive, Shameful, and Unacceptable to them.

ON the other side, the said Prince and Count are persuaded, That the Advantages at this time yielded to the States-General, may hereafter be very prejudicial to themselves, forasmuch as they may put the People of the *Spanish Netherlands* to some dangerous Extremity, considering the Antipathy between the Two Nations; and that extending of Frontiers, is entirely contrary to the Maxims of their Government.

AS to the Upper-Quarter of *Guelder,* the said Prince and Count are of Opinion, That the States-General may be allowed the Power of putting in Garrisons into *Venlo, Ruremond,* and *Steffenswaert,* with Orders to furnish the said *States,* with the Revenues of the Country, which amount to One hundred thousand Florins.

AS to *Bonn,* belonging to the Electorate of *Cologn;* and *Liege* and *Huy,* to the Bishoprick of *Liege;* it is to be understood that these being Imperial Towns, it doth not depend upon the Emperor to consent, that Foreign Garrisons should be placed in them, upon any Pretence whatsoever. But whereas the States-General demand them only for their Security, it is proposed, to place in those Towns a Garrison of Imperial Troops, of whom the *States* may be in no suspicion, as they might be of a Garrison of an Elector, who might possibly have Views opposite to their Interests: But this is propos'd only in case that it shall not be thought more proper to raze one or other of the said Towns.

The Representation *of the* English *Merchants at* Bruges, *relating to the* Barrier-Treaty.

David White, *and other Merchants,* Her Majesty's *Subjects residing at* Bruges, *and other Towns in* Flanders, *crave Leave humbly to represent,*

THAT whereas the Cities of *Lisle, Tournay, Menin, Douay,* and other new Conquests in *Flanders* and *Artois,* taken from the *French* this War, by the united Forces of Her Majesty and Her Allies, are now become entirely under the Government of the States-General; and that we Her Majesty's Subjects may be made liable to such Duties and Impositions on Trade, as the said States-General shall think fit to Impose on us: We humbly hope and conceive, That it is Her Majesty's Intention and Design that the Trade of Her Dominions and Subjects, which is carried on with these new Conquests, may be on an equal Foot with that of the Subjects and Dominions of the States-General, and not be liable to any new Duty, when transported from the *Spanish Netherlands,* to the said new Conquests, as to our great Surprize is exacted from us on the following Goods, *viz.* Butter, Tallow, Salmon, Hides, Beef, and all other Product of Her Majesty's Dominions, which we import at *Ostend,* and there pay the Duty of Entry to the King of *Spain,* and consequently ought not to be liable to any new Duty, when they carry the same Goods, and all others from their Dominions, by a Free Pass or *Transire,* to the said new Conquests: And we are under apprehension that if the said new Conquests be settled or given entirely into the Possession of the States-General for their Barrier, (as we are made believe by a Treaty lately made by Her Majesty's Ambassador, the Lord Viscount *Townshend,* at the *Hague*) that the said States-General may also soon declare all Goods and Merchandises which are Contraband in their Provinces, to be also Contraband or Prohibited in these new Conquests, or new Barrier, by which Her Majesty's Subjects will be deprived of the Sale and Consumption of the following

Products of Her Majesty's Dominions, which are, and have long been, declared Contraband in the *United Provinces*, such as *English* and *Scotch* Salt, Malt Spirits or Corn Brandy, and all other Sorts of Distilled *English* Spirits, Whale and Rape Oil, *&c.* It is therefore humbly conceived, That Her Majesty, out of Her great Care and gracious Concern for the Benefit of Her Subjects and Dominions, may be pleased to direct, by a Treaty of Commerce or some other way, that their Trade may be put on an equal Foot in all the *Spanish Netherlands*, and the new Conquests or Barrier, with the Subjects of *Holland*, by paying no other Duty than that of Importation to the King of *Spain*; and by a Provision, that no Product of Her Majesty's Dominions shall ever be declared Contraband in these new Conquests, except such Goods as were esteemed Contraband before the Death of *Charles* II. King of *Spain*. And it is also humbly prayed, That the Product and Manufacture of the New Conquests may also be Exported without paying any new Duty, besides that of Exportation at *Ostend*, which was always paid to the King of *Spain*; it being impossible for any Nation in *Europe* to Assort an entire Cargo for the *Spanish West-Indies*, without a considerable quantity of several of the Manufactures of *Lisle*, such as Caradoros, Cajant, Picoses, Boratten, and many other Goods, *&c.*

THE chief Things to be demanded of *France* are, To be exempted from Tonnage, to have a Liberty of Importing Herrings and all other Fish to *France*, on the same Terms as the *Dutch* do, and as was agreed by them at the Treaty of Commerce immediately after the Treaty of Peace at *Ryswick*. The enlarging Her Majesty's Plantations in *America*, *&c.* is naturally recommended.

FINIS.

K

SOME REASONS &c.

in a Letter to a

Whig-Lord

SOME

REASONS

TO PROVE,

That no Person is obliged by
his Principles, as a *Whig,*

To Oppose

HER MAJESTY

OR HER

Present Ministry.

In a Letter to a Whig-Lord.

LONDON,

Printed for *John Morphew,* near *Stationers-*
Hall, 1712.   Price 3 *d.*

A

LETTER

TO A

Whig-Lord.

MY LORD,

THE Dispute between your Lordship and Me, hath, I think, no manner of Relation to what, in the common Style of these Times, are called *Principles*; wherein both Parties seem well enough to agree, if we will but allow their Professions. I can truly affirm, That none of the reasonable sober *Whigs* I have conversed with, did ever avow any Opinion concerning Religion or Government, which I was not willing to subscribe; so that, according to my Judgment, those Terms of Distinction ought to be dropped, and others introduced in their stead, to denominate Men, as they are inclined to *Peace* or *War*, to the *Last*, or the *Present Ministry:* For whoever thoroughly considers the matter, will find these to be the only Differences that divide the Nation at present. I am apt to think your Lordship would readily allow this, if you were not aware of the Consequence I intend to draw: For it is plain that the making Peace and War, as well as the Choice of Ministers, is wholly in the Crown; and therefore the Dispute at present lies altogether between those who would support, and those who would violate the Royal Prerogative. This Decision may seem perhaps too sudden and severe, but I do not see how it can be contested. Give me leave to ask your Lordship, whether you are not resolved to oppose the present Ministry to the utmost? and whether it was not chiefly with this design, that upon the opening of the present Session, you gave your Vote against any Peace, till *Spain* and the *West-Indies* were recovered from the *Bourbon* Family? I am confident your Lordship then believed, what several of your House and

Party have acknowledged, that the Recovery of *Spain* was grown impracticable by several Incidents, as well as by our utter Inability to continue the War upon the former foot. But you reasoned right, that such a Vote, in such a Juncture, was the most probable way of ruining the present Ministry. For as Her Majesty would certainly lay much weight upon a Vote of either House, so it was judged that her Ministers would hardly venture to act directly against it; the natural Consequence of which must be, a Dissolution of the Parliament, and a return of all your Friends into a full Possession of Power. This Advantage the Lords have over the Commons, by being a fix'd Body of Men, where a Majority is not to be obtained, but by Time and Mortality, or new Creations, or other Methods, which I will suppose the present Age too virtuous to admit. Several Noble Lords who join'd with you in that Vote, were but little inclined to disoblige the Court, because it suited ill with their Circumstances; but the poor Gentlemen were told it was the safest Part they could act: For it was boldly alledged, that the Queen her self was at the bottom of this Affair; and one of your Neighbours, whom the dread of losing a great Employment often puts into Agonies, was growing fast into a very good Courtier, began to cultivate the chief Minister, and often expressed his Approbation of present Proceedings, till that unfortunate Day of Trial came, when the mighty Hopes of a Change revived his Constancy, and encouraged him to adhere to his old Friends. But the Event, as your Lordship saw, was directly contrary to what your great Undertaker had flatter'd you with. The Queen was so far from approving what you had done, that to shew she was in Earnest, and to remove all future Apprehensions from that Quarter, she took a resolute necessary Step, which is like to make her easy for the rest of her Reign; and which I am confident your Lordship would not have been one of those to have put Her upon, if you had not been most shamefully misinformed. After this your Party had nothing to do, but sit down and murmur at so extraordinary an Exertion of the Prerogative, and quarrel at a Necessity which their own Violence, enflamed by the Treachery of others, had created.

Now, my Lord, if an Action so indisputably in Her Majesty's Power requires any Excuse, we have a very good one at hand: We alledge, that the Majority you *hardly* acquired, with so much Art and Management, partly made up from a *certain transitory Bench*, and partly of those, whose Nobility began with themselves; was wholly formed during the long Power of your Friends, so that it became necessary to turn the Balance, by new Creations; wherein, however, great Care was taken to encrease the Peerage as little as possible, and to make a Choice against which no Objection could be raised, with relation to Birth or Fortune, or other Qualifications requisite for so high an Honour.

THERE is no Man hath a greater Veneration than I, for that Noble Part of our Legislature, whereof your Lordship is a Member; and I will venture to assert, that, supposing it possible for Corruptions to go far in either Assembly, yours is less liable to them than a House of Commons: A standing Senate of Persons, nobly born of great Patrimonial Estates, and of pious learned Prelates, is not easily perverted from intending the true Interest of their Prince and Country; whereas we have found by Experience, that a corrupt Ministry, at the Head of a monied Faction, is able to procure a Majority of whom they please, to represent the People: But then, my Lord, on the other side, if it hath been so contrived by Time and Management, that the Majority of a standing Senate is made up of those who wilfully, or otherwise, mistake the Publick Good; the Cure, by common Remedies, is as slow as the Disease; whereas a good Prince, in the Hearts of his People, and at the Head of a Ministry who leaves them to their free choice, cannot miss a good Assembly of Commons. Now, my Lord, we do assert, that this Majority of yours hath been the Workmanship of above twenty Years: During which time, considering the Choice of Persons, in the several Creations; considering the many Arts used in making Proselites among the young Nobility, who have since grown up; and the wise Methods to prevent their being tainted by University-Principles: Lastly, considering the Age of those who fill up a certain Bench, and with what Views their Successions have been supply'd; I

am surprized to find your Majority so bare and weak, that it is
not possible for you to keep it much longer, unless old Men
be immortal: Neither perhaps would there be any Necessity
to wait so long, if *certain Methods* were put in Practice, which
your Friends have often tried with Success. Your Lordship
plainly sees by the Event, that neither Threats nor Promises
are made use of, where it is pretty well agreed, that they
would not be ineffectual; Voting against the Court, and indeed
against the Kingdom, in the most important Cases, hath not
been followed by the Loss of Places or Pensions, unless in
very few Particulars, where the Circumstances have been so
extreamly aggravating, that to have been passive would have
argued the lowest Weakness or Fear: To instance only in the
Duke of *Marlborough* who against the wholsome Advice of those
who consulted his true Interest, much better than his Flatterers,
would needs put all upon that desperate Issue, of destroying
the present Ministry, or falling himself.

I believe, my Lord, you are now fully convinced, that the
Queen is altogether averse from the Thoughts of ever employing your Party in Her Councils or Her Court. You see a
prodigious Majority in the House of Commons of the same
Sentiments: And the only Quarrel against the Treasurer, is
an Opinion of more Mildness towards your Friends, than it is
thought they deserve; neither can you hope for better Success
in the next Election, while Her Majesty continues her present
Servants, although the Bulk of the People were better disposed to you than it is manifest they are. With all the Advantages I lately mentioned, which a House of Lords has over the
Commons, it is agreed, That the Pulse of the Nation is much
better felt by the latter, than the former, because those represent
the whole People: But your Lordships (whatever some may
pretend) do represent only your own Persons. Now it has
been the old Complaint of your Party, that the Body of Country
Gentlemen always leaned too much (since the *Revolution*)
to the Tory-side: And as your Numbers were much lessened,
about two Years ago, by a very unpopular Quarrel, wherein
the Church thought it self deeply concerned; so you daily
diminish by your Zeal against Peace, which the Landed-

Men, half ruined by the War, do so extreamly want, and desire.

'Tis probable, my Lord, that some Persons may, upon occasion, have endeavoured to bring you over to the present Measures: If so, I desire to know whether such Persons required of you to change any Principles relating to Government, either in Church or State, to which you have been educated? Or did you ever hear that such a Thing was offered to any other of your Party? I am sure neither can be affirmed; and then it is plain, that *Principles* are not concerned in the Dispute. The two chief, or indeed the only Topicks of Quarrel, are, whether the Queen shall chuse Her own Servants? and, whether She shall keep Her Prerogative of making Peace? And I believe there is no Whig in *England* that will openly deny Her Power in either: As to the latter, which is the more avowed, Her Majesty has promised that the Treaty shall be laid before Her Parliament; after which, if it be made without their Approbation, and proves to be against the Interest of the Kingdom, the Ministers must answer for it at their extreamest Peril. What is there in all this that can possibly affect your Principles, as a Whig? Or rather, my Lord, are you not, by all sorts of Principles lawful to own, obliged to acquiesce and submit to Her Majesty upon this Article? But I suppose, my Lord, you will not make a Difficulty of confessing the true genuine Cause of Animosity to be, that those who are *out of Place* would fain be *in*; and that the Bulk of your Party are the *Dupes* of *half a dozen*, who are impatient at their Loss of Power. 'Tis true, they would fain infuse into your Lordship such strange Opinions of the present Ministry, and their Intentions, as none of themselves at all believe. Has your Lordship observed the least Step made towards giving any suspicion of a Design to alter the Succession, to introduce Arbitrary Power, or to hurt the Toleration? unless you will reckon the last to have been damaged by the Bill lately obtained against *Occasional Conformity*, which was your own Act and Deed, by a strain of such profound Policy, and the Contrivance of so profound a Politician, that I cannot unravel it to the Bottom.

Pray, my Lord, give your self leave to consider whence

this indefatigable Zeal is derived, that makes the Heads of your Party send you an hundred Messages, accost you in all Places, and remove Heaven and Earth to procure your Vote upon a Pinch, whenever they think it lies in their way to distress the Queen and Ministry. Those who have already rendred themselves desperate, have no other resource than in an utter Change: But this is by no means your Lordship's Case. While others were at the Head of Affairs, you serv'd the Queen with no more Share in them, than what belonged to you as a Peer, although perhaps you were inclined to their Persons or Proceedings, more than to those of the present Sett: Those who are now in Power, cannot justly blame you for doing so; neither can your Friends out of Place reproach you, if you go on to serve Her Majesty and make Her easy in Her Government, unless they can prove, that unlawful or unreasonable Things are demanded of you. I cannot see how your Conscience or Honour are here concerned; or why People who have cast off all Hopes, should desire you to embark with them against your Prince, whom you have never directly offended. 'Tis just as if a Man who had committed a Murder, and was flying his Country, should desire all his Friends and Acquaintance to bear him Company in his Flight and Banishment. Neither do I see how this will any way answer your Interest; for tho' it should possibly happen that your Friends would be again taken into Power, your Lordship cannot expect they will admit You to the Head of Affairs, or even into the *Secret*. Every thing of Consequence is already bespoke. I can tell you who is to be *Treasurer*, who *Chamberlain*, and who to be *Secretaries*: These Offices, and many others, have been some time fixed; and all your Lordship can hope for, is only the Lieutenancy of a County, or some other honorary Employment, or an Addition to your Title; or, if you were poor, perhaps a Pension. And is not the Way to any of these as fully open at present? And will you declare you cannot Serve your Queen unless you chuse her Ministry? Is this *Forsaking your Principles?* But that Phrase is dropt of late, and they call it *Forsaking your Friends.* To serve your Queen and Country, while any but They are at the Helm, is to *Forsake your Friends.*

This is a new Party-figure of Speech, which I cannot comprehend. I grant, my Lord, that this way of Reasoning is very just, while it extends no farther than to the several Members of their Junto's and Cabals; and I could point out half a score Persons, for each of whom I should have the utmost Contempt, if I saw them making any Overtures to be received into Trust. Wise Men will never be persuaded, that such violent Turns can proceed from Virtue or Conviction: And I believe you and your Friends do in your own Thoughts most heartily despise *that ignominious Example of Apostacy,* whom you outwardly so much caress. But You, my Lord, who have shared no farther in the Favour and Confidence of your Leaders, than barely to be listed of the Party, cannot honorably refuse Serving Her Majesty, and contributing, in your Power, to make her Government easy, though her weighty Affairs be not trusted to the Hands where you would be glad to see them. One Advantage your Lordship may count upon, by acting with the present Ministry, is, that you shall not undergo a State-Inquisition into your Principles, but may believe as you please, in those Points of Government, wherein so many Writers perplex the World with their Explanations. Provided you heartily renounce the Pretender, you may suppose what you please of his Birth; and if you allow Her Majesty's undoubted Right, you may call it Hereditary or Parliamentary, as you think fit. The Ministers will second your utmost Zeal for securing the Indulgence to Protestant Dissenters. They abhor Arbitrary Power as much as You: In short, there is no Opinion properly belonging to you, as a *Whig,* wherein you may not still continue, and yet deserve the Favour and Countenance of the Court; provided you offer nothing in Violation of the Royal Prerogative, nor take the Advantage in critical Junctures to bring Difficulties upon the Administration, with no other View, but that of putting the Queen under the necessity of changing it. But your own Party, my Lord, whenever they return into play, will not receive you upon such easy Terms, although they will have much more need of your Assistance: They will vary their political Catechism as often as they please; and you must answer directly to every Article,

as it serves the present Turn. This is a Truth too visible for
you to call in doubt. How unanimous are you to a Man in
every Point, whether of moment or no! whereas upon Our
Side, many Stragglers have appeared in all Divisions, even
among those who believed the Consequence of their Dissent
would be the worst we could fear: For which, the Courage,
Integrity, and Moderation of those at the Helm, cannot be
sufficiently admired; though I question whether, in good
Politicks, the last ought always to be imitated.

IF your Lordship will please to consider the Behaviour of
the *Tories* during the long Period of this Reign, while their
Adversaries were in Power, you will find it very different
from that of your Party at present. We opposed the Grant to
the Duke of *Marlborough* till he had done something to deserve
so great a Reward; and then it was granted, *nemine contradicente*.
We opposed Repealing the *Test*, which would level the Church
Established, with every sniveling Sect in the Nation. We
opposed the Bill of General Naturalization, by which we were
in danger to be over-run by Schismaticks and Beggars: The
Scheme of breaking into the Statutes of Colleges, which
obliged the Fellows to take holy Orders; the Impeachment of
Dr. *Sacheverill*; the hopeful Project of limiting Clergymen what
to Preach; with several others of the same Stamp, were stren-
uously opposed, as manifestly tending to the Ruin of the
Church. But you cannot give a single Instance, where the
least Violation hath been offered to Her Majesty's undoubted
Prerogative, in either House, by the Lords or Commons of
Our Side. We should have been glad indeed to have seen
Affairs in other Management; yet, we never attempted to bring
it about by stirring up the City, or inviting Foreign Ministers
to direct the Queen in the Choice of Her Servants, much less
by infusing Jealousies into the next Heir: Endeavours were not
publickly used to blast the Credit of the Nation, and discourage
Foreigners from Trusting their Money in our Funds: Nor were
Writers suffered openly, and in Weekly Papers, to revile
Persons in the highest Employments. In short, if you can
prove where the Course of Affairs, under the late Ministry, was
any way clogged by the Church-Party, I will freely own the

latter to have so far acted against Reason and Duty. Your Lordship finds I would argue from hence, that even the warmest Heads on your Side, and those who are deepest engaged, have no tolerable Excuse for thwarting the Queen upon all Occasions; much less You, my Lord, who are not involved in their Guilt or Misfortunes, nor ought to involve your self in their Resentments.

I HAVE often wondered with what Countenance these Gentlemen, who have so long engrossed the greatest Employments, have shared among them the Bounties of the Crown and the Spoils of the Nation, and are now thrown aside with universal Odium, can accost others, who either never received the Favours of the Court, or who must depend upon it for their daily Support; with what Countenance, I say, these Gentlemen can accost such Persons in their usual Style, *My Lord, you were always with us; you will not forsake your Friends: You have been still right in your Principles: Let us join to a Man, and the Court will not be able to carry it.* And this frequently in Points where *Whig* and *Tory* are no more concerned, than in the length or colour of your Perriwigs? Why all this Industry to ply you with Letters, Messages and Visits, for carrying some peevish Vote, which only serves to display inveterate Pride, ill Nature and Disobedience, without effect? Though you are flattered it must possibly make the Crown and Ministry so uneasy, as to bring on the necessity of a Change: Which however is at best a Design but ill becoming a good Subject, or a Man of Honour. I shall say nothing of those who are fallen from their heights of Power and Profit, who then think all claim of Gratitude for past Favours is cancelled: But you, my Lord, upon whom the Crown has never cast any peculiar Marks of Favour or Displeasure, ought better to consider the Duty you owe your Sovereign, not only as a Subject in general, but as a Member of the Peerage, who have been always the strenuous Asserters of just Prerogative, against popular Encroachments, as well as of Liberty, against Arbitrary Power: So that it is something unnatural, as well as unjust, for one of your Order, to oppose the most Mild and Gracious Prince that ever reigned, upon a Party-Picque, and in Points where Prerogative was never disputed.

But after all, if there were any probable Hopes of bringing Things to another Turn by these violent Methods of your Friends, it might then perhaps be granted, that you acted at least a politick Part: But surely the most Sanguine among them could hardly have the Confidence to insinuate to your Lordship, the Probability of such an Event, during Her Majesty's Life. Will any Man of common Understanding, when he has recovered his Liberty, after being kept long in the strictest Bondage, return of his own Accord to Gaol, where he is sure of being confined for ever? This Her Majesty and Millions of her Subjects, firmly believe to be exactly the Case; and whether it be so or no, 'tis enough that it is so believed: And this Belief is attended with as great an Aversion for those Keepers, as a good Christian can be allowed to entertain, as well as with a Dread of ever being again in their Power: So that whenever the Ministry may be changed, it will certainly not be to the Advantage of your Party, except under the next Successor, which I hope is too remote a View for your Lordship to proceed by; though I know some of your Chiefs, who build all their Expectations upon it.

For indeed, my Lord, your Party is much deceived, when they think to distress a Ministry for any long Time, or to any great Purpose, while those Ministers act under a Queen who is so firmly convinced of their Zeal and Ability for Her Service, and who is at the same time so thoroughly possessed of Her Peoples Hearts. Such a Weight will infallibly at length bear down the Balance: And, according to the Nature of our Constitution, it ought to be so; because, when any one of the Three Powers whereof our Government is composed, proves too strong for the other Two, there is an End of our Monarchy. So little are you to regard the crude Politicks of those who cried out, *The Constitution was in Danger*, when Her Majesty lately encreased the Peerage; without which it was impossible the two Houses could have proceeded, with any Concert, upon the most weighty Affairs of the Kingdom.

I know not any Quarrels your Lordship, as a Member of

the *Whig*-Party, can have against the Court, except those which I have already mentioned; I mean, the Removal of the late Ministry, the Dismission of the Duke of *Marlborough* and the present Negotiations of Peace. I shall not say any thing farther upon these Heads; only, as to the second, which concerns the Duke of *Marlborough* give me leave to observe, that there is no Kingdom or State in *Christendom*, where a Person in such Circumstances, would have been so gently treated. But it is the Misfortune of Princes, that the Effects of their Displeasure, are frequently much more publick than the Cause: The Punishments are in the Face of the World, when the Crimes are in the Dark: And Posterity, without knowing the Truth of Things, may perhaps number us among the ungrateful Populace of *Greece* and *Rome*, for discarding a General, under whose Conduct our Troops have been so many Years Victorious: Whereas it is most certain, that this great Lord's Resolution against Peace upon any Terms whatsoever, did reach the Ministry at home as much as the Enemy abroad: Nay, his Rage against the former was so much the more violent of the two, that, as it is affirmed by skilful Computors, he spent more Money here upon *Secret Service*, in a few Months, than he did for many Years in *Flanders*. But whether that be true or false, your Lordship knows very well, that he resolved to give no Quarter, whatever he might be content to take, when he should find himself at Mercy. And the Question was brought to this Issue, Whether the Queen should dissolve the present Parliament, procure a new one of the *Whig*-stamp, turn out those who had ventured so far to rescue her from Insolence and ill Usage, and invite her old Controllers to resume their Tyranny, with a recruited Spirit of Vengeance? Or, Whether she should save all this Trouble, Danger, and Vexation, by only changing one General for another?

WHATEVER good Opinion I may have of the Present Ministry, I do not pretend, by any thing I have said, to make your Lordship believe that they are Persons of sublime abstracted *Roman* Virtue: But, where two Parties divide a Nation, it so usually happens, that although the Virtues and Vices may be pretty equal on both sides, yet the publick

L

Good of the Country may suit better with the private Interest of one Side than of the other. Perhaps there may be nothing in it but Chance; and it might so have happened if Things were to begin again, that the *Junto* and their Adherents would have found it their Advantage to be obedient Subjects, faithful Servants, and good Church-men. However, since these Parts happen to be acted by another Sett of Men, I am not very speculative, to enquire into the Motives; but having no Ambition at Heart, to mislead me, I naturally side with those who proceed most by the Maxims wherein I was educated. There was something like this in the Quarrel between *Cæsar* and *Pompey: Cato* and *Brutus* were the two most virtuous Men in *Rome*; the former did not much approve the Intentions of the Heads on either side; and the latter, by Inclination, was more a Friend to *Cæsar:* But, because the Senate and People generally followed *Pompey*, and that *Cæsar*'s Party was only made up of the Troops with which he Conquered *Gaul*, with the Addition of some profligate Deserters from *Rome*; those two excellent Men, who thought it base to stand Neuter where the Liberties of their Country was at stake, joined heartily on that side which undertook to preserve the Laws and Constitution, against the Usurpations of a victorious General, whose Ambition was bent to overthrow them.

I CANNOT dismiss your Lordship, without a Remark or two upon the Bill for appointing Commissioners to enquire into the Grants, since 1688. which was lately thrown out of your House, for no other Reason, than the hopes of putting the Ministry to a Plunge. It was universally known that the Lord Treasurer had prevailed to wave the Tack in the House of Commons, and promised his Endeavours to make the Bill pass by it self in the House of Lords. I could name at least, five or six of your Noble Friends, who, if left to the Guidance of their own Opinion, would heartily concur to an entire Resumption of those Grants; others assure me they could name a dozen; yet, upon the hope of weakening the Court, perplexing the Ministry, and shaking the Lord Treasurer's Credit in the House of Commons, You went on so unanimously, that I do not hear there was one single Negative, in your whole List, nor above one *Whig*-Lord guilty of a *Suspicious Absence*; who, being much in your Lordships Circumstances, of a great Patrimonial Estate, and under no Obligations to either side, did not think himself bound to forward a Point, driven on meerly to make the Crown uneasy at this Juncture, while it no way affected his Principles as a *Whig,* and which I am told was directly against His private Judgment. How he hath since been treated as an Apostate and Betrayer of his Friends, by some of the Leaders and their Deputies among you, I hope your Lordship is ashamed to reflect on; nor do I take such open and sudden Declarations to be very wise, unless you already despair of his Return, which, I think, after such Usage, you justly may. For the rest, I doubt your Lordship's Friends have missed every End they proposed to themselves in rejecting that Bill: My Lord Treasurer's Credit is not any way lessened in the House of Commons. In your own House you have been very far from making a Division among the Queen's Friends, as appeared manifestly a few days ago, when you lost your Vote by so great a Majority, and disappointed those who had been encouraged to hire Places, upon certain Expectations of seeing a Parade to the *Tower.* Lastly, it may probably happen, that those who opposed an Inquisition into the Grants, will be found to have hardly done any very great Service to the present Possessors: To charge those Grants with six Years Purchase to the Publick, and then to confirm the Title by Parliament, would in effect be no real Loss to the Owners, because by such a Confirmation, they would rise in value proportionably, and differ as much as the best Title can from the worst. The adverse Party knew very well that nothing beyond this was intended; but they cannot be sure, what may be the Event of a second Inspection, which the Resentment of the House of Commons will probably render more severe, and which you will never be able to avert, when your Number lessens, as it certainly must; and when the Expedient is put in Practice, without a Tack, of making those Grants part of a Supply. From whence it is plain that the Zeal against that Bill, arose in a great measure from some other Cause, than a Tenderness to those who were to suffer by it.

I shall conclude, my Lord, with putting you in mind, that you are a Subject of the Queen, a Peer of the Realm, and a Servant of your Country; and in any of these Capacities, you are not to consider what you dislike, in the Persons of those who are in the Administration, but the manner of conducting themselves while they are in. And then I do not despair, but your own good Sense will fully convince you, that the Prerogative of your Prince, without which Her Government cannot subsist; the Honour of your House, which hath been always the great Asserter of that Prerogative; and the Welfare of your Country, are too precious to be made a Sacrifice to the Malice, the Interest, and the Ambition of a few Party-Leaders.

FINIS.

A HUE AND CRY
AFTER DISMAL

A Hue and cry after Dismal;

Being a full and true Account, how a Whig *Lord was taken at* Dunkirk, *in the Habit of a Chimney-sweeper, and carryed before General* Hill.

WE have an old Saying, *That it is better to play at small Game than to stand out:* And it seems, the Whigs practice accordingly, there being nothing so little or so base, that they will not attempt, to recover their Power. On Wednesday Morning the 9th Instant, we are certainly informed, that Collonell Killegrew (who went to France with Generall Hill) walking in Dunkirk Streets met a tall Chimney-Sweeper with his Brooms and Poles, and Bunch of Holly upon his Shoulders, who was followed by another of a shorter Size. The Tall Fellow cry'd in the French Language (which the Collonel understands) Sweep, Sweep; The Collonell thought he knew the Voice, and that the Tone of it was like one of your fine Speakers. This made him follow the Chimney-Sweeper, and examine nicely his Shape and Countenance. Besides, he conceived also that the Chimney-Sweeper's Man was not altogether unknown to him, so the Collonel went to wait on the Generall who is Governor of Dunkirk for Her Majesty, and told his Honor, that he had a strong Suspicion that he had seen Dismal in the Streets of Dunkirk. (Now you must know, that our Courtiers call a certain great Whig Lord by the Name of Dismal; belike, by reason of his dark and dismal Countenance). That is impossible sure, said the Governor. I am confident of it said the Collonel; nay, and what is more, the Fellow that followed him was Mr. Squash, tho' the Master was as black as his Man; and if your Honor pleases, I will bring them both to you immediately, for I observed the House they went in. So, away went the Collonel with a File of Musquiteers, and found them both in an Ale-house, that was kept by a Dutch-man. He could see nothing of the Master, but a Leg upon each Hobb, the rest of the Body being out of sight, the Collonel ordered him to come down, which he did, with a great heap of Soot after him. Master and Man were immediately conducted through the Town, with a great Mob at their Heels to the Governor's Castle, where his Honor was sitting in a Chair with his English and French Nobles about him. The Governor with a stern Countenance asked the tall Man who he was! He answered he was a Savoyard, (for beyond Sea, all the Chimney-Sweepers come from Savoy, a great Town in Italy) and he spoke a sort of Gibberish like broken French. But the French Mounseers that were by, assured the Governor, he could be no French-man, no nor Savoyard neither. So then the Governor spoke to him in English, said there was Witnesses ready to prove, that under pretence of sweeping Chimnyes cheaper than other People, he endeavored to persuade the Townsfolks not to let the English come into the Town, and how as that he should say, that the English would cut all the French-mens Throats, and that his Honor believed he was no Chimny-Sweeper (though that was too good a Trade for him) but some Whiggish English Traitor. The Governor then gave Command, that both of them should be washed in his Presence by two of his Guards. And first they began with the Man, and spent a whole Pail full of Water in vain: Then they used Soap and Suds, but all to no Purpose; at last they found he was a Black-a-more, and that they had been acting the Labor-in-vain. Then the Collonel whispered the Governor, your Honor may plainly see that this is Squash. (Now you must know, that Squash is the Name of a Blackamore that waits upon the Lord whom the Courtiers call Dismal). Then with a fresh Pail they began to wash the Master; but for a while, all their Scrubbing did no good; so that they thought he was a Black-amoor too. At last they perceived some dawning of a dark sallow Brown; and the Governor immediately knew it was the Lord Dismal, which the other, after some shuffling Excuses, confessed. The Governor then said, I am sorry to see your Lordship in such a Condition, but you are Her Majesty's Prisoner, and I will send you immediately to England, where the Queen my Liege may dispose of you according to Her Royal Pleasure. Then his Honor ordered new Cloaths to be made both for Master and Man, and sent them on Shipboard: From whence in a few Hours they landed in England.

It is observed, that the Lord's Face, which at best is very Black and Swarthy, hath been much darker ever since, and all the Beauty-washes he uses, it is thought will never be able to restore it. Which wise Men reckon to be a just Judgment on him for his late Apostacy.

A Letter
from the Pretender
to a Whig-Lord

A LETTER from the
PRETENDER,
To a Whig-Lord.

My Lord W——,   S. Germain, July 8. 1712.

I Thank you heartily for your Letter; and you may be firmly assured of my Friendship. In Answer to what you hint, that some of our Friends suspect; I protest to you, upon the Word of a King, and my Lord *Middleton* will be my Witness, that I never held the least Correspondence with any one Person of the *Tory* Party: I observe, as near as I can, the Instructions of the King my Father, among whose Papers there is not one Letter, as I remember, from any *Tory*, except two Lords and a Lady, who, as you know, have been for some Years past devoted to Me and the *Whigs*. I approve of the Scheme you sent me, sign'd by our Friends. I do not find 24's Name to it: Perhaps he may be sick, or in the Country. *Middleton* will be satisfied to be Groom of the Stole; and if you have *Ireland*, 11 may have the Staff, provided 15 resigns his Pretensions; in which Case, he shall have 6000 *l.* a Year for Life, and a Dukedom. I am content 13 should be Secretary, and a Lord; and I will pay his Debts when I am able. I confess I am sorry your General Pardon has so many Exceptions; but you, and my other Friends, are better Judges of that. It was with great Difficulty I prevailed on the Queen to let me Sign that Commission for Life, tho' her Majesty is entirely reconciled. If 2 will accept the Privy-Seal, which you tell me is what would please him, the Salary shall be doubled: I am obliged to his good Intentions, how ill soever they have succeeded. All other parts of your Plan I entirely agree with; only as to the Party that opposeth us, your Proposal about Z may bring an Odium upon my Government: He stands the first Excepted; and we shall have enough against him in a legal

way. I wish you would allow me twelve more Domesticks of
my own Religion, and I will give you what Security you please,
not to hinder any Designs you have of altering the present
Establish'd Worship. Since I have so few Employments left
me to dispose of, and that most of our Friends are to hold
theirs for Life; I hope you will all be satisfied with so great a
share of Power. I bid you heartily Farewel, and am Your
assured Friend,

James R.

Lord *Wharton*'s

LETTER

TO THE

Lord Bishop of S. *Asaph*.

Price Two Pense.

A
LETTER

OF

THANKS

FROM MY

Lord *Wharton*

TO THE

Lord Bᵖ of S. *Asaph*,

In the Name of the

Kit-Cat-Club.

Printed in the Year 1712.

M

My LORD,

IT was with no little Satisfaction I undertook the pleasing Task, assigned me by the Gentlemen of the *Kit-Cat-Club*, of addressing your Lordship with Thanks for your late Service so seasonably done to our Sinking Cause, in reprinting those most excellent Discourses, which you had formerly preached with so great Applause, though they were never heard of by us, till they were recommended to our Perusal by the *Spectator*, who some time since, in one of his Papers, entertained the Town with a Paragraph out of the *Post-Boy*, and your Lordship's extraordinary *Preface*.

THE World will perhaps be surprized, that Gentlemen of our Complexion, who have so long been piously employed in overturning the Foundations of Religion and Government, should now stoop to the puny Amusement of reading and commending Sermons: But your Lordship can *work* Miracles, as well as *write* on them; And I dare assure your Lordship, and the World, that there is not an Atheist in the Whole Kingdom (and we are no inconsiderable Party) but will readily subscribe to the Principles so zealously advanced, and so learnedly maintained in those Discourses.

I CANNOT but observe with infinite Delight, that the Reasons your Lordship gives for reprinting those immortal Pieces, are urged with that Strength and Force, which is peculiar to your Lordship's Writings, and is such, as all who have any Regard for Truth, or Relish for good Writing, must admire, though none can sufficiently commend. In a word, the Preface is equal to the Sermons, less than That ought not, and more cannot, be said of it. In this you play the Part of a Prophet, with the same Address as that of a Preacher in those; and, in a Strain no ways inferior to *Jeremiah*, or any of those old Pretenders to Inspiration, sagely foretell those impending Miseries which seem to threaten these Nations, by the Introduction of Popery and Arbitrary Power: This a Man of less Penetration than your Lordship, without a Spirit of Divination, or going to the Devil for the Discovery, may justly *fear and presage from the natural Tendency of several Principles and*

Practices which have of late been so studiously revived: I know your
Lordship means those long-since exploded Doctrines of
Obedience, and Submission to Princes, which were only
calculated to make *a Free and Happy People Slaves and Miserable.*
Who but Asses, and Pack-Horses, and Beasts of Burden, can
entertain such servile Notions? What! Shall the Lives and
Liberties of a Free-born Nation be sacrificed to the Pride and
Ambition, the Humour and Caprice of any one single Person?
Kings and Princes are the Creatures of the People, meer
State-Pageants, more for Shew than Use: And shall we fall
down and worship those Idols, those Golden Calves of our
own setting up? No, never by G—d, as long as I can hold a
Sword, or your Lordship a Pen.

'Twas suitable to that admirable Foresight, which is so
conspicuous in every Part of your Lordship's Conduct, to
take this effectual Method of delivering yourself *from the*
Reproaches and Curses of Posterity, by publickly declaring to all the
World, that though, in the constant Course of your Ministry, you have
never failed, on proper Occasions, to recommend the Loving, Honouring,
and Reverencing the Prince's Person, so as never to break His
Royal Shins, nor tread upon His Heels; yet you never intended
Men should pay any Submission or Obedience to Him any
longer than He acted according to the Will and Pleasure of His
People. This you say is the Opinion of CHRIST, St. *Peter,*
and St. *Paul:* And 'faith I am glad to hear it; for I never
thought the Prigs had been Whigs before: But since your
Lordship has taught them to declare for Rebellion, you may
easily persuade them to do as much for Prophaneness and
Immorality; and then they, together with your Lordship,
shall be enrolled Members of our Club. Your Lordship, a
little after, (I suppose, to strengthen the Testimony of the
aformention'd Authors) takes Care to tell us, that *this always*
was, and still is, your own Judgment in these Matters. You need
not fear we should suspect your Constancy and Perseverance;
for my Lord *Sommers,* that great Genius, who is the Life and
Soul, the Head and Heart of our Party, has long since observed,
that we have never been disappointed in any of our Whig

Bishops, but they have always unalterably acted up, or, to speak properly, down to their Principles.

It is impossible for me, My Lord, in this short Address, to do Justice to every Part of your incomparable Preface: Nor need I run riot in Encomium and Panegyrick, since you can perform that Part so much better for yourself; for you only give those Praises, which you only can deserve; as you have formerly proved, in the Dedication of your *Essay upon Miracles*, to Dr. *Godolphin*, where you declare your Work to be the most perfect of any upon that Subject, in order to pay a very uncommon Complement to your Patron, by telling Him you had prevailed with your Modesty to say so much of your Performance, because you would not be thought to make so ill a Complement to him, as to present him with what you had not a great Esteem for yourself.

Tho' I can't go thro' the whole Preface, yet I think myself obliged in Gratitude to thank your Lordship in a more particular Manner for the last Part of it, where you display the Glories of the Whig Ministry in such strong and lasting Colours, as must needs chear and refresh the Sight of all Whig Spectators, and dazzle the Eyes of the Tories. Here, your Lordship rises, if possible, above yourself: Never was such Strength of Thought, such Beauty of Expression, so happily joined together. Heavens! Such Force, such Energy in each pregnant Word! Such Fire, Such Fervour, in each glowing Line! One would think your Lordship was animated with the same Spirit with which our Hero fought. Who can read, un-mov'd, these following Strokes of Oratory? *Such was the Fame, Such was the Reputation, Such was the Faithfulness and Zeal, to Such a Height of Military Glory, Such was the Harmony and Consent, Such was the Blessing of God*, &c. O! the irresistible Charm of the Word *Such*! Well, since *Erasmus* wrote a Treatise in Praise of Folly; and my Lord *Rochester* an excellent Poem upon *Nothing*, I am resolved to employ the *Spectator*, or some of his Fraternity, (Dealers in Words) to write an Encomium upon SUCH. But whatever Changes our Language may undergo (and every thing that is *English* is given to change) this happy Word is sure to live in your immortal Preface.

Your Lordship does not end yet, but to crown all, has another such in Reserve, where you tell the World, *We were just entring on the Ways that lead to Such a Peace, as would have answer'd all our Prayers*, &c. Now, perhaps, some snarling Tory might impertinently enquire, when we might have expected such a Peace? I answer, when the *Dutch* could get nothing by the War, nor we Whigs lose any thing by a Peace; or to speak in plain Terms, (for every one knows I am a free Speaker as well as a free Thinker) when we had exhausted all the Nation's Treasure, (which every body knows could not have been long first) and so far enrich'd ourselves, and beggar'd our Fellow-Subjects, as to bring them under a Necessity of Submitting to what Conditions we should think fit to impose; and this too we should soon have effected, if we had continued in Power. But alas! just in that critical Juncture, when (as we thought) our Designs were ripe for Execution, the Scene changed, *God, for our Sins*, as your Lordship wisely observes, *permitted the Spirit of Discord* (that is the Doctrine of Obedience and Submission to Princes) *to go forth, and by troubling the Camp, the City, and the Country, (and Oh that it had spared the Places Sacred to his Worship) to spoil, for a Time, this Beautiful and Pleasing Prospect, and give us in its Stead, I know not what. . . .* Oh Exquisite! How pathetically does your Lordship complain of the Downfal of Whiggism, and *Daniel Burges*'s Meeting-house! The generous Compassion your Lordship has shewn upon this tragical Occasion, makes me believe your Lordship will not be unaffected with an Accident that had like to have befallen a poor Whore of my Acquaintance about that Time, who being big with Whig, was so alarmed at the Rising of the Mob, that she had like to have miscarried upon it; for the Logical Jade presently concluded, (and the Inference was natural enough) that if they began with pulling down Meeting-houses, it might end in demolishing those Houses of Pleasure, where she constantly paid her Devotion; and, indeed, there seems a close Connexion between *Extempore* Prayer and *Extempore* Love. I doubt not, if this Disaster had reach'd your Lordship before, you would have found some Room in that moving *Parenthesis*, to have express'd your Concern for it.

I come now to that last Stroke of your Lordship's almighty Pen; I mean that expressive Dash — which you give when you come to the New Ministry, where you break off with an artful *Aposiopesis*, and by refusing to say any Thing of them yourself, leave your Readers to think the worst they possibly can. Here your Lordship shews yourself a most consummate Orator, when even your very Silence is thus eloquent.

Before I take my Leave, I cannot but congratulate your Lordship upon that distinguishing Mark of Honour which the House of Commons has done your Preface, by ordering it to be burnt. This will add a never-failing Lustre to your Character, when future Ages shall read, how a few Pages of your Lordships could alarm the Representative Body of the Nation. I know your Lordship had rather live in a Blaze, than lie buried in Obscurity; and would, at any rate, purchase Immortality tho' it be in Flames. Fire being a mounting Element, is a proper Emblem of your Lordship's aspiring Genius.

I shall detain your Lordship no longer, but, according to your Example, conclude with a short Prayer; (tho' Praying, I confess, is not my Talent) May you never want Opportunities of thus signalizing yourself, but be *transmitted to Posterity*, under the Character of one who dares sacrifice every Thing that is most dear to you (even your own darling Labours) to promote the Interest of our Party, and stand sainted in the Whig-Kalendar, as a Martyr for the Cause. This is the sincere Wish of the greatest (next yourself) of your Lordship's Admirers,

Wharton.

FINIS.

Remarks on
Fleetwood's Preface

Vol. II.   Numb. 34.

The EXAMINER.

From **Thursday** *July* 17, to **Thursday** *July* 24. 1712.

Ecce iterum Crispinus ——

THE Bishop of St. *Asaph*'s famous *Preface* having been
so much buffetted of late between Advocates and
Opposers, I had a Curiosity to inspect some of his other
Works. I sent to the Booksellers in *Duck-Lane* and *Little-
Britain*, who returned me several of the Sermons which
belonged to that *Preface*; among others, I took notice of that
upon the Death of the Duke of *Glocester*, which had a little
Preface of its own, and was omitted, upon mature Deliberation,
when those Sermons were gathered up into a Volume; tho'
considering the Bulk, it could hardly be spared. It was a great
Masterpiece of Art in this admirable Author, to write such a
Sermon, as, by help of a *Preface*, would pass for a *Tory* Discourse
in one Reign, and by omitting that *Preface*, would denominate
him a *Whig* in another: Thus by changing the Position, the
Picture represents either the *Pope* or the *Devil*, the *Cardinal*
or the *Fool*. I confess it was malicious in me, and what few
others would have done, to rescue those Sermons out of their
Dust and Oblivion; without which, if the Author had so
pleased, they might have passed for new Preached as well as
new Printed. Neither would the former *Preface* have risen up
in judgment to confound the latter. But upon second
Thoughts, I cannot tell why this *willfully* forgotten *Preface*
may not do the Reverend Author some Service. It is to be
presumed that the *Spectator* published the last with that Intent;
why therefore should not my publishing the first be for the
same end? And I dare be confident, that the part I have chosen
will do his Lordship much more Service; for here it will be
found, that this Prelate did, once in his Life, think and write
as became him; and that while he was a private Clergyman, he

could print a *Preface* without fear of the Hangman. I have chose to set it at length, to prevent which might be objected against me, as an unfair Representer; should I reserve any part of this admirable Discourse, as well as to imitate the judicious *Spectator*, tho' I fear I shall not have such goodly Contributions from our Party as that Author is said to have from another upon the like Occasion; or if I chance to give offence, be promised to have my Losses made up to me, for my great Zeal in circulating *Prefaces:* Without any such deep and politick Designs, I give it to the World out of meer good Nature, that they may find what Conceptions the worthy Author has formerly had of things, when his Business was yet undone; so to silence *a clamorous Party*, who, from the late Preface, are too apt, how unjustly soever, to conclude, his Lordships Principles are not agreeable to his Preferments.

THE Bishop of St. *Asaph*'s first Preface, to a Sermon Preached upon the Death of the Duke of *Gloucester*.

I *Give this Sermon up to the desires of a great many good People of the Parishes of St.* Austin *and St.* Dunstan *in the West, to whom I can deny nothing of this Nature which they shall find reasonable to ask of me; but not to their desires only, but also to the hopes I have, that from something or other hinted at in it, other wise and virtuous People may be put upon Considering whereabouts we are, and on Contributing all that lies in them to the preventing whatever Evils we may apprehend from the great Loss we have sustained in the Death of the most Noble and most hopeful Prince the Duke of* Gloucester. *I know I have no other Aims than these, in making this Sermon publick; and they who know me well will, I believe, think so too: I undertake not therefore to defend the Irregularity of some of my Thoughts, nor the Order in which they are ranged; they were produced in Grief and deep Concern, and that I think may, in some sort, excuse them with tender and good-natured People. I am only careful of guarding against two sorts of Men;* 1. *Such as will needs call this great Misfortune, a* Judgment of God, *for what has past amongst us.* 2. *Such as will certainly try to make it one, as soon as ever they can. To the first, we must freely own, we have deserved*

God's greatest Judgments, but not for the Causes they Assign; and freely own that this Misfortune has the face of one, and is as heavy as a Judgment; and therefore I hope all People will improve under it, and make as good use of it, as if it were indeed a Judgment. But till they shall produce some certain and impartial Rules by which they proceed in forming Censures, and in applying them to Nations, or to private People, they will give us leave, I hope, to suspend. And to the second sort, who think to turn a Kingdom into a Commonwealth, I can only say, that I hope the Extent of our Dominions, the Number of our Nobility, the Honour of our Gentry, the Genius of our People, and the whole Current of our Laws, will always provide us with a ready Answer to an impudent and clamorous Faction. God, I hope, will evermore preserve us from a Species of Government, as ill fitted for our Nation, as Popery is for our Religion.

IN this excellent Preface, the worthy Author thought fit to charge the *Fanaticks* and *Whigs*, upon the Duke of *Glocester's* Death, as People that would *try to make it a Judgment of God upon us for our Sins, by turning the Kingdom into a Commonwealth.* The Satyr must certainly be determined to them; for neither the *Tories* or *Nonjurors* were ever charged with such Principles, but rather as carrying the *Regal* Authority too high, asserting the Divine Right of Kings. This *Species of Government*, which the Learned Prelate says, is *as ill fitted for our Nation as Popery is for our Religion*, was by some People, it seems, endeavoured to be brought in, whom he terms an *impudent and clamorous Faction.* Whether that *impudent and clamorous Faction* would really do all those things he charges them with, is, by the *Whigs*, denied, and charitable Men may in part make a Question; but that by this, he did, and could then only mean the *Whigs*, could be no Question at all; since none else were ever charged with those Crimes in these Kingdoms; and they have always been so, tho' seldom indeed so heavily, unless by high-flying *Tories* or *Jacobites.* It seems his Lordship had dreadful Apprehensions of what they would *certainly do*, and *begs of God evermore to preserve us from this Species:* And surely he was in the right, for that would be, indeed, *giving us we know not what*—His Lordship's Enemies *will tell the rest with Pleasure!*

Appendix to
Conduct and *Remarks*

The EXAMINER.

From **Monday** *January* 12, to **Friday** *January* 16, 1712.

Nihil est aliud in Fædere, *nisi ut Pia & æterna* Pax *sit.*
Cicero pro C. Balbo.

I BEGIN to think, that tho' perhaps there may be several very exact *Maps* of *Great Britain* to be had at the Shops in *Amsterdam* or the *Hague*, and some shining *Genii* in that Country can, it may be, look out the most remarkable Places in our Island, especially those upon the Sea-Coast, or near it, as *Portsmouth, Chatham, Torbay*, and the like; yet it is highly necessary, that *Chamberlayne*'s Present *State*, or some other good Book of that Sort, were carefully Translated into *Dutch, In usum Illustrissimorum Ordinum*, or with any other Sounding and pompous Title, only signifying, That it was done for the Use of our Good Allies, and to set them right in the Nature of our Government, Constitution and Laws; with which they do not appear to be so well acquainted as might be expected. I am sensible, that as things now stand, if a *Manifesto* or *Memorial* should be sent them, humbly representing to their *High Mightinesses*, That *Great Britain* is an Independent Monarchy, govern'd by its own Laws: That the *Queen* is Supream over all Orders of the Realm: That no other Prince, Prelate, State or Potentate, hath or ought to have any Authority and Jurisdiction over us: That where the *Queen*, *Lords* and *Commons*, solemnly consent, it is a Law; and where the collective Body of the People agree, it is the Sense of the Nation: That the making War and Peace is the Prerogative of the Crown; and, That all Alliances are to be observed only so far as they answer the Ends for which they were made: In such a Case, 'tis not unlikely, but the *Amsterdam Gazette*, or some other *Paper* in the *Seven Provinces*, would immediately Answer all this by publickly protesting, That it came from the *Jacobites* and *Frenchify'd High-Fliers*, and therefore ought not to be admitted as Genuine: For of late that Celebrated Writer, and two or three of his Seconds, have undertaken to tell us poor *Britains*, who are our best Subjects, and how we ought to behave ourselves towards our Allies. So that in this unhappy Juncture, I do not see when we shall come to a right Understanding. On the other hand, suppose we agreed to give them the Precedence, and left the first Proposal for Overtures of Accommodation to their Management; this perhaps might quickly bring us to be better acquainted. Let them therefore lay aside all clumsie Pretences to Address; tell us no more of former Battles, Sieges and Glories; nor make Love to us in Prose, and extol our Beauty, our Fortune, and their own Passion for us, to the Stars: But let them come roundly to the Business, and in plain Terms give us to understand, That they will not Recognize any other Government in *Great Britain*, but *Whigarchy* only: That they treated with us as such, and are not oblig'd to acknowledge an Usurp'd Power call'd a *Monarchy*, to which they are utter Strangers: That they have a just Demand upon us ever since the *Revolution*; which is a Precedent for their Interposing, whenever Popery and Arbitrary Power are coming in upon us, which at present, they are inform'd by their Friends, is our Case: And besides they are advised by able Council, That we are only *Tenants* for *Life*, and they being mention'd in the *Entail*, are oblig'd to have a watchful Eye over us, and to see that neither *Waste* nor *Dilapidation* be done upon the Premises. If all this be not the Case, and a true State of the Controversie, as I heartily hope it is not, I leave any Rational Creature, pick him where you will between the *Danube* and *Ganges*, to judge of the following *Remonstrance*.

A WAR is undertaken by several Potentates in Conjunction, upon certain Causes and Conditions, plainly express'd in a Writing call'd *The Grand Alliance*. This War is carried on with Success; the Enemy offers to Treat, and proposes to satisfie all the just Demands of the several Parties engag'd against them. *Great Britain* makes her Claim, so doth *Portugal*; and both are fully satisfied. The *Dutch* produce their *Barrier* of *Gertruydenberg*, and are assur'd they shall have it, except two or three Places at most. *Savoy* and *Prussia* have more than ever they ask'd. Only the *Emperor* will have all *Spain*, contrary to the Reasons upon which his *Brother*'s Renuntiation was founded, and in direct Violation of a fundamental Maxim, *The Ballance of Power*; so that he would involve us in a *Second* War, and a new *Grand Alliance*, under pretence of observing the old one. This, in short, is the Case; and yet, after all the Bloodshed, Expence and Labour, to compass these great Ends, tho' *Her Britannick Majesty* finds by Experience that every Potentate in the Grand Alliance, except Her Self, has actually broke it every Year; tho' She stands possess'd of an undoubted Right to make Peace and War; tho' she has pro-cur'd for Her Allies all that She was oblig'd to by Treaty; tho' Her Two *Houses* of *Parliament* humbly entreat Her to finish the great Work; tho' Her People with one Voice admire and congratulate the wise Steps she has taken, and cry loud to Her to defer their Happiness no longer; tho' some of the *Allies*, and *One* or *Two* of the *Provinces* have declar'd for Peace, and Her Majesty's Domestick Enemies dread it, as the utter Downfal of their Faction; yet still the Blessing depends, and Expectation is our Lot. The *Menacing Pensionary* has Scruples; he desires time to look out for something else to Demand: There are a Dozen or two of *Petty Princes*, who want Silk Stockings, and Lace round their Hats; we must stay till the *Second Part* of *Denain* comes upon the Stage, and Squire *South* promises to go directly to *Madrid*, the next time we shew him the way thither.

HER *Majesty* is all Goodness and Tenderness to Her People and Her *Allies*. A brighter Example of Piety could not adorn the Life of *Her Royal Grandfather*, whose solemn *Anniversary* we must shortly Celebrate. She has now Prorogu'd the best *Parliament* that ever Assembled in Her Reign, and Respited Her own Glory, and the Wishes, Prayers, and Wants of Her People, only to give some of Her *Allies* an opportunity to think of the Returns they owe Her, and try if there be such a Thing as Gratitude, Justice, or Humanity in *Europe*. This

Conduct of *Her Majesty* is without Parallel. Never was so great a Condescention made to the unreasonable Clamours of an Insolent Faction, now dwindled to the most Contemptible Circumstances. It is certainly high time they should begin to meditate other Measures, unless they vainly imagine the Government must part with both its Attributes of Mercy and Justice, till they are pleased to be Dutiful and Obedient. What ill-grounded Hopes and Expectations they have under-hand Administer'd to any of the *Allies*, is not worth my while to enquire; since whatever they are, they must come attended with the blackest Treason and Ingratitude. The *Dutch* have the least Reason in the World to rely on such a broken Reed; and after having solemnly promised to conform themselves to *Her Majesty*'s Wisdom, and depend on Her Conduct, which is the Language of their latest Professions; such clandestine Management would fully deserve all those Appellations, with which the Writings of the *Whigs* are so richly Embelish'd.

AFTER all, when *Her Majesty* and Her Subjects have waited one Period more, and affixt a new Date to their Wishes and their Patience; since Peace is the only End of every Alliance, and since all that we fought for is yielded up by the Enemy, in Justice to her *Prerogative*, to her *Parliament*, and her *People*, the desirable Blessing will, no doubt, be reach'd out to us: Our Happiness will not be put off, till they, who have Ill-will at us, can find Time and Power to prevent it. All that a stubborn Ally can then expect, is Time to come in, and accept those Terms which himself Once thought Reasonable. The present Age will soon taste the Sweets of such Conduct, and Posterity as highly applaud it. Only they, who now Rail and Calumniate, will do so still, and who are dispos'd to give every thing the same Treatment which makes for our Safety and Wellfare, and spoils their Game of Disorder and Confusion.

'TIS true, the present stagnation of Affairs is accounted for another way; and the Party give out, that *France* begins to draw back, and would explain several Articles upon us: But the Authors of this Forgery know very well I do not miscall it; and are Conscious to the Criminal Reasons, why it is with so much Industry bandy'd about. *France* rather enlarges her

Offers, than abates or recedes from them: So happy are we, in finding our most Inveterate and Ungenerous Enemies within our own Bowels! The *Whigs*, according to Custom, may Chuckle and Solace themselves with the visionary Hopes of Coming Mischief, and imagine they are grown Formidable, because they are to be humour'd in their Extravagancies, and to be paid for their Perverseness. Let them go on to Glory in their projected Schemes of Government, and the blessed Effects they have produc'd in the World. 'Twas not enough for them to make *Obedience* the Duty of the Sovereign, but this *Obedience* must at length be made *Passive*; and that *Non-resistance* may not wholly vanish from among the Vertues, since the Subject is weary of it, they would fairly make it over to their Monarch. The *Compact* between Prince and People is suppos'd to be mutual: but *Grand Alliances* are, it seems, of another nature: a failure in one Party does not disengage the rest; they are tied up and entangled, so long as any one Confederate adheres to the *Negative*; whilst we are not allow'd to make use of the *Polish* Argument, and plead *Non Loquitur*. But these Artifices are too thin to hold: They are the Cobwebs which the *Faction* have spun out of the last Dregs of their Poison, made to be swept away with the unnecessary Animals who contrived them. Their Tiranny is at an end, and their Ruin very near: I can only advise them to become their Fall, like *Cæsar*, and *Die with Decency*.

Refutation of Falsehoods
against Lewis

Vol. III.   Numb. 21.

The EXAMINER.

From **Friday** *January* 30, to **Monday** *February* 2, 1712.

Beware of Counterfeits, for such are abroad.   Saffold's *Quack-Bill.*

Quin, quæ dixisti modo,
Omnia ementitus equidem Sosia Amphytrionis sum.   Plaut.

Parva metu primo, mox sese attollit in auras.   Virg.

I Intend this Paper for the Service of a particular Person;
but herein, I hope, at the same time, to do some Service
to the Publick. A Monstrous Story hath been for a while
most industriously handed about, reflecting upon a Gentleman
in great Trust, under the Principal Secretary of State; who
hath Conducted himself with so much Prudence, that, before
this Incident, neither the most virulent Pens nor Tongues
have been so bold to attack him. The Reader easily understands, that the Person here meant is Mr. *Lewis*, Secretary to
the Earl of *Dartmouth*, concerning whom a Story hath run, for
about Ten Days past, which makes a mighty Noise in this
Town, is no doubt with very ample Additions transmitted to
every Part of the Kingdom, and probably will be return'd to
us by the *Dutch Gazetteer*, with the Judicious Comments
peculiar to that Political Author: Wherefore having received
the Fact and the Circumstances from the best Hands, I shall
here set them down before the Reader, who will easily pardon
the Style, which is made up of Extracts from the Depositions
and Assertions of the several Persons concerned.

ON *Sunday* last was Month, Mr. *Lewis*, Secretary to the *Earl*
of *Dartmouth*, and Mr. *Skelton*, met by Accident at Mr. *Scar-*
borough's Lodgings in St. *James*'s, among Seven other Persons,
viz. the Earls of *Sussex* and *Finlatter*, the Lady *Barbara Skelton*,
Lady *Walter*, Mrs. *Vernon*, Mrs. *Scarborough*, and Miss *Scar-*

borough her Daughter; who all declar'd, that Mr. *Lewis* and Mr. *Skelton* were half an Hour in Company together. There Mrs. *Scarborough* made Mr. *Skelton* and Mr. *Lewis* known to each other; and told the former, that he ought to thank Mr. *Lewis* for the Trouble he had given himself in the dispatch of a Licence, under the *Privy Seal*, by which Mr. *Skelton* was permitted to come from *France* to *England*. Hereupon Mr. *Skelton* saluted Mr. *Lewis*, and told him, he would wait on him at his House to return him his Thanks. Two or three Days after, Mr. *Skelton*, in Company with the Earl of *Sussex*, his Lady's Father, went to a House in *Marlborough-street*, where he was inform'd Mr. *Lewis* liv'd; and as soon as the supposed Mr. *Lewis* appear'd, Mr. *Skelton* express'd himself in these Words; *Sir, I beg your Pardon*; *I find I am mistaken: I came to visit Mr.* Lewis *of my Lord* Dartmouth's *Office, to thank him for the Service he did me in passing my* Privy Seal. Mr. *Levi* alias *Lewis* answer'd, *Sir, There is no Harm done:* Upon which Mr. *Skelton* immediately withdrew to my Lord *Sussex*, who stay'd for him in the Coach, and drove away. Mr. *Skelton*, who was a Stranger to the Town, order'd the *Coachman* to drive to Mr. *Lewis*'s without more particular Directions, and this was the occasion of the Mistake.

For above a Fortnight nothing was said of this Matter; but on *Saturday* the 24th of *January* last, a Report began to spread, that Mr. *Skelton*, going by Mistake to Mr. *Henry Levi* alias *Lewis*, instead of Mr. *Lewis* of the *Secretary's Office*, had told him, *That he had Services for him from the* Earls *of* Perth, Middleton, Melfort, *and about Twelve Persons more of the* Court of St. Germains. When Mr. *Lewis* heard of this, he writ to the above-mentioned *Henry Levi* alias *Lewis*, desiring to be inform'd, what ground there was for this Report; and receiv'd for Answer, *That his Friend* Skelton *could best inform him*. Mr. *Lewis* writ a second Letter, insisting on an Account of this Matter, and that he would come and demand it in Person. Accordingly he and *Charles Ford*, Esq; went the next Morning, and found the said *Levi* in a great Surprise at the Report, who declared, *He had never given the least occasion for it*; *and that he would go to all the* Coffee-houses *in Town, to do Mr.* Lewis *Justice*. He was ask'd by Mr. *Lewis*, whether Mr. *Skelton* had named from what Places and Persons he had brought those Services? Mr. *Levi* alias *Lewis* answered, *He was positive Mr.* Skelton *had neither nam'd Person nor Place.* Here Mr. *Skelton* was call'd in, and *Mr. Levi* alias *Lewis* confirm'd what he had said in his Hearing. Mr. *Lewis* then desir'd, he would give him in Writing what he had declar'd before the Company; but Mr. *Levi* alias *Lewis* excus'd it as unnecessary, because he had already said, He would do him Justice in all the *Coffee-houses* in Town. On the other Hand, Mr. *Lewis* insisted to have it in Writing, as being less troublesome; and to this Mr. *Levi* alias *Lewis* reply'd, *That he would give his* Answer *by* Three a Clock *in the Afternoon.* Accordingly Mr. *Ford* went to his House at the Time appointed, but did not find him at home; and in the mean time the said *Levi* went to *White*'s *Chocolate-House*, where notwithstanding all he had before denied, he spread the above-mentioned Report afresh, with several additional Circumstances, as that when Mr. *Skelton* and the Earl of *Sussex* came to his House, they stay'd with him a considerable time, and drank Tea.

THE Earl of *Peterborough*, Uncle to the said Mr. *Skelton*, thought himself oblig'd to enquire into the Truth of this Matter; and after some search, found Mr. *Levi* alias *Lewis* at the *Thatch'd-House Tavern*, where he deny'd every thing again to *his* Lordship, as he had done in the Morning to Mr. *Ford*, Mr. *Lewis*, and Mr. *Skelton*.

THIS Affair coming to the Knowledge of the *Queen*, Her *Majesty* was pleas'd to order an Examination of it by some *Lords* of the *Council*. Their *Lordships* appointed *Wednesday* the 28th of *January* last for this Enquiry; and gave notice for Attendance to the said *Levi* alias *Lewis*, and several other Persons who had knowledge of the Matter. When Mr. *Levi* alias *Lewis* was call'd in, he declar'd, *That Mr.* Skelton *told him he had Services for him from* France, *but did not name any Persons. William Pulteney*, Esq; who was summoned, affirmed, *That he had told him*, Mr. Skelton *nam'd the Earl of* Perth *and* Melfort. *Levi* alias *Lewis* appear'd in some Confusion; for he had intreated Mr. *Pulteney*, not to say he had named any Names, *For he would not stand to it*; but Mr. *Pulteney* answer'd, *You may give yourself the Lie*; *I won't.* The Earl of *Sussex* declar'd, he did not go out of his Coach, and that his Son-in-law, Mr. *Skelton*, had not been gone half a Minute before he return'd to the Coach. Mr. *Skelton* declar'd, That he knew Mr. *Lewis* by sight perfectly well; that he immediately saw his mistake; that he said nothing to him but the Words first mentioned; and that he had not brought Mr. *Lewis* any Service from any Person whatsoever. The Earl of *Finlatter*, and other Persons summon'd, declar'd, That Mr. *Lewis* and Mr. *Skelton* were Personally known to each other, which render'd it wholly Improbable that Mr. *Skelton* should mistake him: So that the whole Matter appear'd to be only a foolish and malicious Invention of the said *Levi* alias *Lewis*, who, when called to an Account, utterly disown'd it.

I f Mr. *Levi*'s View, in broaching this incoherent Slander, was to make his Court to any particular Persons, he has been extreamly disappointed, since all Men of Principle, laying aside the Distinction of Opinions in Politicks, have entirely agreed in abandoning him; which I observe with a great deal of Pleasure, as it is for the Honour of Humane-kind. But as neither Virtue nor Vice are wholly engross'd by either Party, the good Qualities of the Mind, whatever Byass they may receive by mistaken Principles, or mistaken Politicks, will not be extinguish'd. When I reflect on this, I cannot, without being a very partial Writer, forbear doing Justice to *William Pulteney*, Esq; who being desired by this same Mr. *Levi*, to drop one part of what he knew, refused it with Disdain. Men of Honour will always side with the Truth; of which the Behaviour of Mr. *Pulteney*, and of a great number of Gentlemen of Worth and Quality, are undeniable Instances.

I A M only sorry, that the unhappy Author of this Report, seems left so entirely Desolate of all his Acquaintance, that he hath nothing but his own Conduct to direct him; and consequently is so far from acknowledging his Iniquity and Repentance to the World, that in the *Daily Courant* of *Saturday* last, he hath Publish'd a *Narrative*, as he calls it, of what pass'd between him and Mr. *Skelton*, wherein he recedes from some part of his former Confession. This *Narrative* is drawn up by way of Answer to an Advertisement in the same Paper two Days before: Which Advertisement was couch'd in very moderate Terms, and such as Mr. *Levi* ought, in all Prudence, to have acquiesced in. I freely acquit every Body but himself from any Share in this miserable Proceeding, and can foretel him, that as his prevaricating Manner of adhering to some part of the Story, will not convince one Rational Person of his Veracity; so neither will any Body interpret it, otherwise than as a Blunder of a helpless Creature, left to it self; who endeavours to get out of one Difficulty, by plunging into a greater. It is therefore for the sake of this poor young Man, that I shall set before him, in the plainest manner I am able, some few Inconsistences in that *Narrative* of his; the Truth of which, he says, he is ready to attest upon Oath; which, whither he would avoid, by an Oath only upon the Gospels, himself can best determine.

MR. *Levi* says, in this aforesaid Narrative in the *Daily Courant, That Mr.* Skelton, *mistaking him for Mr.* Lewis, *told him he had several Services to him from* France, *and nam'd the Names of several Persons, which he* [Levi] *will not be positive to.* Is it possible, that among several Names, he cannot be positive so much as to *One,* after having nam'd the Earls of *Perth, Middleton* and *Melfort,* so often at *White*'s and the *Coffee-houses?* Again, He declar'd, that my Lord *Sussex* came in with Mr. *Skelton;* that both drank Tea with him, and therefore whatever Words pass'd, my Lord *Sussex* must be a Witness to: But his Lordship declares before the Council, That he never stirr'd out of the Coach; and that Mr. *Skelton,* in going, returning, and talking with *Levi,* was not absent half a Minute: Therefore, now in his printed Narrative, he contradicts that essential Circumstance of my Lord *Sussex* coming in along with Mr. *Skelton,* so that we are here to suppose that this Discourse past only between him and Mr. *Skelton,* without any Third for a Witness, and therefore he thought he might safely affirm what he pleas'd. Besides, the nature of their Discourse, as Mr. *Levi* reports it, makes this part of his Narrative impossible and absurd, because the Truth of it turns upon Mr. *Skelton*'s mistaking him for the real Mr. *Lewis;* and it happens that seven Persons of Quality were by in a Room, where Mr. *Lewis* and Mr. *Skelton* were half an Hour in Company, and saw them talk together. It happens likewise, that the Real and Counterfeit *Lewis*, have no more resemblance to each other in their Persons, than they have in their Understandings, their Truth, their Reputation, or their Principles. Besides in this Narrative, Mr. *Levi* directly affirms what he directly deny'd to the Earl of *Peterborow*, Mr. *Ford*, and Mr. *Lewis* himself; to whom he twice or thrice expresly affirm'd, That Mr. *Skelton* had not nam'd either Place or Person.

THERE is one Circumstance in *Levi*'s Narrative which may deceive the Reader. He says Mr. *Skelton* was taken into the Dining-Room; this Dining-Room is a Ground-Room next the Street, and Mr. *Skelton* never went further than the Door of it. His many Prevarications in this whole Affair, and the many thousand various ways of telling his Story, are too tedious to be related. I shall therefore conclude with one Remark. By the true Account given in this Paper it appears, that Mr. *Skelton*, finding his mistake before he spake a Word, begg'd Mr. *Levi*'s Pardon, and by way of Apology told him, His Visit was intended to Mr. *Lewis* of my Lord *Dartmouth*'s Office, to thank him for the *Service* he had done him, in passing the Privy Seal. It is probable that Mr. *Levi*'s low Intellectuals were deluded by the Word *Service*, which he took as Complements from some Persons, and then it was easie to find Names: Thus, what his Ignorance and Simplicity misled him to begin, his Malice taught him to propagate.

I HAVE been the more Sollicitous to set this Matter in a clear Light, because Mr. *Lewis* being employ'd and trusted in Publick Affairs, if this Report had prevail'd, Persons of the first Rank might possibly have been wounded through his Sides.

ADDRESS TO THE QUEEN

The Humble

ADDRESS

Of the Right Honourable the

Lords Spiritual and Temporal

In Parliament Assembled,

PRESENTED TO

HER MAJESTY

On *Saturday* the Eleventh Day of *April*, 1713.

WITH

Her Majesties

MOST GRACIOUS

ANSWER.

LONDON,
Printed by *John Baskett*, Printer to the Queens most Excellent Majesty, And by the Assigns of *Thomas New-
comb*, and *Henry Hills*, deceas'd. 1713.

(Price One Peny)

o

[1713 april 9]

Ordered that an humble Address be made to Her Majesty, to return the most
humble thanks of this House to Her Majesty, for the most gracious Speech from the
Throne, and for Her Majesty's communicating to this House that a Peace is
agreed on, and to congratulate Her Majesty upon the Success of her Endeavours
for a generall Peace and for what she Her Majesty has Done to secure the
Protestant Succession; and to Assure Her Majesty, that if she is pleased
to express her Dependence next under God upon the Duty and Affection of her
People, this House will make all Return from that are Due from obedient
Subjects to the most indulgent Sovereign

The Humble

ADDRESS

Of the Right Honourable the

Lords Spiritual and Temporal

In PARLIAMENT Assembled.

Die Veneris 10 *Aprilis,* 1713.

Most Gracious Sovereign,

WE Your Majesties most Dutiful and Loyal Subjects, the Lords Spiritual and Temporal in Parliament Assembled, Do, with the greatest Joy and Satisfaction, Return our humble Thanks to Your Majesty for Your most Gracious Speech from the Throne, and for Communicating to Your Parliament that a Peace is Concluded; by which we hope, with the Blessing of God, that Your People will, in few Years, Recover themselves after so Long and Expensive a War; And also do Congratulate Your Majesty upon the Success of Your Endeavours for a General Peace.

We never had the least Doubt, but that Your Majesty, who is the great Support and Ornament of the Protestant Religion, would Continue to take, as You have always done, the Wisest Measures for Securing the Protestant Succession, towards which nothing can be more Necessary than the perfect Friendship there is between Your Majesty and the House of *Hanover.*

And we do humbly Assure Your Majesty, That as You Express Your Dependence, next under God, upon the Duty and Affection of Your People, we think our selves Bound by the strictest Tyes of Religion, Loyalty, and Gratitude, to make all the Dutiful Returns that can be paid, by the most Obedient Subjects to the most Indulgent Sovereign.

FINIS.

APPENDIXES

THE
Publisher's PREFACE

to SOME ADVICE HUMBLY OFFERED TO THE MEMBERS OF THE OCTOBER CLUB

ABOUT the Year when her late Majesty, of Blessed Memory, thought proper to change her Ministry, and brought in Mr. *Harley*, Mr. *St. John*, Sir *Simon Harcourt*, and some others: The first of these being made an Earl and Lord Treasurer, he was soon after blamed by his Friends for not making a general Sweep of all the *Whigs*, as the latter did of their Adversaries, upon her Majesty's Death, when they came into Power. At that Time a great Number of Parliament Men amounting to above two hundred, grew so warm upon the Slowness of the Treasurer in this Part, that they formed themselves into a Body under the Name of the *October* Club, and had many Meetings, to consult upon some Methods that might spur on those in Power, so that they might make a quicker Dispatch, in removing all of the *Whig*-Leaven from the Employments they still possessed. To prevent the ill Consequences of this Discontent among so many worthy Members; the rest of the Ministry joined with the Treasurer, partly to pacify, and partly to divide those who were in greater Haste than moderate Men thought convenient. It was well known, that the supposed Author met a considerable Number of this Club in a publick House, where he convinced them very plainly of the Treasurer's Sincerity, with many of those very Reasons which are urged in the following Discourse, besides some others which were not so proper to appear at that Time in Print.

The Treasurer alledged in his Defence, that such a Treatment would not consist with Prudence, because there were many Employments to be bestowed, which required Skill and Practice; that several Gentlemen who possessed them, had been long versed, and very loyal to her Majesty, and had never been violent Party-men, and were ready to fall into all honest Measures for the Service of their Queen and Country. But however, as Offices became vacant, he would humbly recommend to her Majesty such Gentlemen whose Principles with Regard both to Church and State, his Friends would approve of, and he would be ready to accept their Recommendations. Thus, the Earl proceeded in procuring Employments for those who deserved them by their Honesty, and Abilities to execute them; which, I confess to have been a Singularity not very likely to be imitated. However, the Gentlemen of this Club, still continued uneasy that no quicker Progress was made in Removals, until those who were least violent began to soften a little, or by dividing them, the whole Affair dropped. During this Difficulty, we have been assured, that the following Discourse was very seasonably published with great Success, shewing the Difficulties that the Earl of *Oxford* lay under, and his real Desire, that all Persons in Employments should be true loyal Churchmen, zealous for her Majesty's Honour and Safety, as well as for the Succession in the House of *Hanover*, if the Queen should happen to die without Issue. This Discourse having been published about the Year 1711, and many of the Facts forgotten, would have not been generally understood without some Explanation, which we have now endeavoured to give, because it seems a Point of History too material to be lost. We owe this Piece of Intelligence to an Intimate of the supposed Author.

It's Out at Last:

OR,

French Correspondence

Clear as the SUN.

THere is a Story goes of an old Prophetess, that Prophesied always true to no purpose; for her Fate was, never to be *believ'd*: The same thing has happen'd, to a worthy Patriot and Member of the House of *Commons*, who has openly in his Speeches declar'd that he was sure that the M——stry *Corresponded* with *France*, and that in a little time there would appear manifest Proofs of it; but such is the Stupidity or rather Malignancy of the *Tory*-Party, that they took no manner of notice of what this Eloquent Gentleman warn'd them of, in his pathetick Harangues, 'till now that they have a convincing Proof of it, with a witness, in this treacherous Surrender of *Dunkirk*.

It is judiciously observed by a learned Author, that the Fate of Princes and States is very hard; for Plots against them are never believ'd 'till they are executed, and consequently without the possibility of being prevented, for every-body will allow me, that what is already executed, is so. I am afraid this will be soon verify'd upon this Nation, by the Clandestine giving up of that Important Place.

I take it, that the Surrender of *Dunkirk* is so plain a proof of our M——stry's Corresponding with *France*, that I should pity any Man, as oppressed with a political Lethargy, should he doubt of it any more: I say this as well to vindicate the Honour of that worthy Gentleman, as to awaken this insensible drousy Nation, who cannot perceive that it is Day when the Sun shines.

It was pleasantly said by a *Swedish* Poet,

Timeo Danos Dona ferentes.

I am afraid of the *Danes* when they bring Presents.

Let us only consider the value of this Present of the *French* Monsieur; the many Millions it has cost him; the many more it has cost us: It is not only giving us a strong Fortification, but Fleets of Frigats and Privateers, and all Pretences afterwards to disturb our Trade in the Channel, and all this is still doubted when it is taken from him, and given to us: And can any Man imagine he does all this for nought? If any Man can show me that ever he did the like before, I will yield the point; but if no such Instance can be given, it must follow demonstratively, that he reckons the present M——stry his Friends: for give me leave to say, no Man would make such a valuable Present but to a Friend, and it were very unbecoming for any but a Friend to accept of it: Therefore I wish the Pa——ent would make the M——stry give an account if they came honestly by it.

I have often ruminated in my Mind, of the Reasons that have induc'd the F——h Monsieur to make this Surrender; and I will give you my Conjectures in short. I think, in the first place, it is not altogether improbable that he has Sold it now, as he Bought it before; and I wish that may not be the chief Reason of the Scarcity of Species at this time. *2dly*, I believe he has done it out of pure spight to the *Whigs*, whom he knows to be his irreconcileable Enemies; and I will be bold to say, if he had been studying for it, he could not have serv'd them a more malicious spightful Trick. *3dly*, Why may it not be a Token of Love to the *Tories*, and particularly to my Lady M——sham, for the great Service she has done him: and I am the more confirm'd in my Opinion, since the Governor has been nam'd.

Let us now consider the Difference between the Old and the New M——stry: They scorn'd to accept of *Dunkirk* and a dozen more strong Towns of the *French* King, when they were offer'd; a plain and convincing Proof that they had no secret Dealings with *France*. The D. of M——gh scorn'd that modern Frenchify'd way of taking of Towns; he scorn'd so pitiful a Conquest, without Powder and Bullets, Blood and Wounds. By the same uncorrupt and generous Temper, they refus'd a Sum of Money which the F——h King offer'd them to help to drive the D. of *Anjou* out of *Spain*. *It shall never be said that England took French Money*, was the Saying of a Great and a Wise Minister; a Saying which ought to be Engrav'd in Letters of Gold upon his Tomb-stone. O the miserable Condition of the Nation, that has been forc'd to part with so uncorrupt, so wise, and so truly an *English* M——ry! Men that, for their own Ends, are carrying on private Bargains with our Enemies; in pursuance of which, they have not only accepted of *Dunkirk*, but would, without any manner of Hesitation, take *Toulon* and St. *Malo* too, if they were offer'd.

Thus I think it is plain, from what has been said, that our M——ry are in a close Correspondence with *France*; and, that the F——h Monsieur expects Justice from them, not to say some little Favour to boot. I wish the Nation had open'd their Eyes before it was too late, and consider'd well before they had any Dealings with the Devil; for it is well known, that when once he has drawn them in to accept of the least Trifle as a Present, they are his for ever after.

PREFACE
to FOUR SERMONS
by WILLIAM, Lord Bishop of St. ASAPH

THE Publishing a few Sermons, whilst I live, the latest of which was preach'd above eight Years since, and the first above seventeen, will make it very natural for People to inquire into the Occasion of doing so: And to such I do very willingly assign these following Reasons.

First, From the Observations I have been able to make, for these many Years last past, upon our publick Affairs; and from the natural Tendency of several Principles and Practices, that have, of late, been studiously revived, and from what has followed thereupon, I could not help both fearing and presaging, that these Nations would, some Time or other, if ever we should have an enterprizing Prince upon the Throne, of more Ambition than Virtue, Justice, and true Honour, fall into the Way of all other Nations, and loose their *Liberty*.

Nor could I help foreseeing, to whose Charge, a great deal of this dreadful Mischief, whenever it should happen, would be laid, whether justly or unjustly was not my Business to determine; but I resolved, for my own particular Part, to deliver my self, as well as I could, from the Reproaches and the Curses of Posterity, by publickly declaring to all the World, that altho' in the constant Course of my Ministry, I have never failed, on proper Occasions, to recommend, urge, and insist upon, the loving, honouring, and the reverencing the Princes Person, and holding it, according to the Laws, inviolable and sacred, and paying all Obedience and Submission to the Laws, tho' never so hard and inconvenient to private People: Yet did I never think my self at Liberty, or authorized, to tell the People, that either *Christ*, St. *Peter*, or St. *Paul*, or any other holy Writer, had, by any Doctrine delivered by them, subverted the *Laws* and *Constitutions* of the Country, in which they lived or put them in a worse Condition, with Respect to their Civil

Liberties, than they would have been, had they not been Christians. I ever thought it a most impious Blasphemy against that Holy Religion, to father any thing upon it, that might encourage Tyranny, Oppression, or Injustice, in a Prince; or that easily tended to make a free, and happy People, *Slaves*, and *miserable*. No: People may make themselves as wretched as they will; but let not God be called into that wicked Party. When Force, and Violence, and hard Necessity, have brought the Yoak of Servitude upon a Peoples Neck, Religion will supply them with a patient and submissive Spirit under it, 'till they can innocently shake it off: But certainly Religion never puts it on. This always was, and this at present is, my Judgment of these Matters: And I would be transmitted to Posterity (for the little share of Time such Names as mine can live) under the Character of one who loved his Country, and would be thought a *good Englishman*, as well as a *good Clergyman*.

This Character I thought would be transmitted, by the following Sermons, which were made for, and preached in a private Audience, when I could think of nothing else but doing my Duty on the Occasions that were then offer'd by God's Providence, without any manner of Design of making them publick: And, for that Reason, I give them now, as they were then delivered. By which I hope to satisfie those People who have objected a Change of Principles to Me, as if I were not now the same Man I formerly was. I never had but one Opinion of these Matters; and that I think is so reasonable and well grounded, that I believe I never can have any other.

Another Reason of my publishing these Sermons, at this time, is, that I have a Mind to do my self some Honour, by doing what Honour I could to the Memory of Two most excellent Princes, and who have very highly deserved at the Hands of all the People of these Dominions, who have any true Value for the *Protestant Religion*, and the *Constitution* of the *English Government*, of which they were the great *Deliverers*, and *Defenders*. I have lived to see their illustrious Names very rudely handled, and the great Benefits they did this Nation, treated slightly, and contemptuously. I have lived to see our Deliverance from *Arbitrary Power*, and *Popery*, traduced and vilified by some who formerly thought it was their greatest Merit, and made it Part of their Boast and Glory, to have had a little Hand and Share in bringing it about: And others who, without it, must have lived in Exile, Poverty, and Misery, meanly disclaiming it, and using ill *the Glorious Instrument* thereof. Who could expect such a Requital of such Merit? I have, I own it, an Ambition of exempting my self from the Number of *unthankful* People. And as I loved and honoured those Great Princes living, and lamented over them when dead, so I would gladly raise them up a Monument of Praise, as lasting as any Thing of mine can be; and I choose to do it at this Time, when it is so unfashionable a Thing to speak honourably of them.

The Sermon that was preached upon the *Duke of Gloucester's* Death, was printed quickly after, and is now, because the Subject was so suitable, joyn'd to the others. The Loss of that most promising and hopeful Prince was, at that Time, I saw, unspeakably great; and many Accidents since have convinced us, that it could not have been over-valued. That precious Life, had it pleased God to have prolonged it to the usual Space, had saved us many Fears, and Jealousies, and dark Distrusts, and prevented many Alarms, that have long kept us, and will keep us still, waking and uneasy. Nothing remained to comfort and support us, under this heavy Stroke, but the Necessity it brought the King and Nation under, of settling the *Succession* in the House of HANOVER, and giving it an *Hereditary Right*, by *Act* of *Parliament*, as long as it continues *Protestant*. So much good did God, in his merciful Providence, produce from a Misfortune, which we could never otherwise have sufficiently deplored.

The fourth Sermon was preached upon the *Queen's Accession* to the Throne, and in the first Year in which that Day was solemnly observed (for by some Accident or other, it had been over-looked the Year before) and every one will see, without the Date of it, that it was preached very early in this Reign, since I was able only to *promise* and *presage* its future Glories and Successes, from the good Appearances of Things, and the happy Turn our Affairs began to take; and could not then count up the Victories and Triumphs that, for seven Years after, made it, in the Prophets Language, *a Name, and a Praise among all the People of the Earth.* Never did seven such Years together pass over the Head of any *English Monarch,* nor cover it with so much Honour: The Crown and Sceptre seemed to be the *Queen*'s least Ornaments. Those, other Princes wore in common with her: And Her great Personal Virtues were the same before, and since. But such was the Fame of her Administration of Affairs at home; such was the Reputation of her Wisdom and Felicity in choosing Ministers; and such was then esteemed their Faithfulness and Zeal, their Diligence and great Abilities in executing Her Commands: To such a Height of Military Glory did her Great *General* and her *Armies* carry the *British* Name abroad: Such was the Harmony and Concord betwixt Her and Her *Allies*: And such was the Blessing of God upon all Her Councels and Undertakings, that I am as sure as History can make Me, no Prince of Ours was ever yet so prosperous and successful, so loved, esteemed, and honoured, by their Subjects and their Friends, nor near so formidable to their Enemies. We were, as all the World imagined then, just entring on the Ways that promised to lead to such a Peace, as would have answered all the Prayers of our Religious Queen, the Care and Vigilance of a most able Ministry, the Payments of a willing and obedient People, as well as all the glorious Toils and Hazards of the Soldiery; when God, for our Sins, permitted *the Spirit of Discord* to go forth, and, by troubling sore the Camp, the City, and the Country, (and oh that it had altogether spared the Places sacred to his Worship!) to spoil, for a Time, this beautiful and pleasing Prospect; and give us, in its Stead, I know not what—our Enemies will tell tell the rest with Pleasure. It will become Me better to pray to God to restore us to the Power of obtaining such a Peace, as will be to his Glory, the Safety, Honour, and the Welfare of the Queen and her Dominions, and the general Satisfaction of all Her High and Mighty Allies.

MAY, 2.

1712.

Swift's Contributions to 'The Post Boy' and 'The Evening Post'

I. *The Post Boy*, Dec. 25–27, 1711

London, Dec. 27. On Saturday the 22d instant, about Four in the Morning, Mrs Anne Long, sister of Sir James Long, Bart. died at Linn in Norfolk, after a Sickness but of Four Hours. She was a Lady very much celebrated here for her Beauty, Virtue, and good Sense; and is extremely lamented by all who knew her.

II. *The Evening Post*, November 11–13, 1712

London, Nov. 12. We have received a more particular Account relating to the Box sent to the Lord Treasurer, as mention'd in our last, which is as follows.

On the Third Instant a tall, slender Boy, having on a Gray Coat and a brown bob Peruke, delivered a Band-Box, (directed to the Lord Treasurers Porter) at a Penny-Post House behind Ludgate, which the next Morning was carried to the Office in Chichester Rents, Chancery Lane, and from thence to the Lord Treasurers by one Carson, a Penny Post man, in which upon opening was found another* Band-Box, directed to the Lord Treasurer. The Box was carry'd up to my Lord's Bed-Chamber, and deliver'd to his Lordship, who† lifting up the Lid as far as the Pack-thread that ty'd it would give way, said, He saw a Pistol; whereupon, a Gentleman in the Room desired the Box might be given to him; he took it to the Window, at some Distance from my Lord, and open'd it, by cutting with

---

* From this point, the account printed in the *Post-Boy*, for the same date, is identical, except for occasional differences of spelling and punctuation. It was introduced thus:

London, Nov. 13. *The Truth of the Fact concerning the Band-Box sent to the* Lord-Treasurer, *we are inform'd, is as followeth*:

On Tuesday Morning, the 4th Instant, the Penny-Post-Man deliver'd a small Parcel at the Lord-Treasurer's House, directed to his Lordship's Porter, in which, upon opening, was found enclos'd a Band-Box, *etc.*

† lifting] stretching *Post-Boy*.

a Pen-knife the Pack-threads that fasten'd the Lid. The first Thing that appear'd was the Stock and Lock of a Pocket-Pistol, lying across the middle of the Band-Box, and fasten'd at each end with two Nails; on each side of the Fire-lock were laid the Middle-pieces of two large Ink-horns charg'd with Powder and Ball, and Touch-holes bored at the Butt-ends of 'em, to which were fasten'd two Linnen Bags of Gunpowder, and at the other end of the Bags were two Quils fill'd with Wildfire. These two artificial Barrels were plac'd with the Muzzels contrary-ways, and the Quil of one of 'em directed to the Pan of the Pistol, as the other probably was, tho' disorder'd by the Carriage. The Gentleman, who open'd the Box, apprehending some Mischief was intended, would not touch the Pistol-stock till he had remov'd all the other Machines; then gently widening the Box, the Nails which fastned the Stock at either end gave Way. He found the Fire-lock prim'd and cock'd, and a Piece of Thread fastned to the Trigger, which he conceiv'd he had cut in the opening. The small Nails which fasten'd the Stock at either end, were so contriv'd, That by taking it up at the first View, as it was natural to do with all the Implements about it, the Cock would have gone down and fir'd the whole Train, which would have immediately discharged both Barrels, different Ways; this could not have been avoided, had the Pistol-stock been pull'd out with any Force, before the Nails were loosen'd, and the Thread cut which was tied to the Trigger.

III. *The Post Boy*, November 15–18, 1712

London, Nov 18. On Saturday Morning last, about 7 of the Clock, the Duke of Hamilton and the Lord Mohun fought a Duel in Hide-Park; his Grace's Second was Col. Hamilton, and his Lordship's Major-Gen. Mackartney. The Lord Mohun died on the Spot; and my Ld Duke soon after he was brought home, who receiv'd the following Wounds, one on the Right side of his Leg, about 7 inches long; another in his Right Arm; the third, in the upper part of his Left Breast, running down-wards into his Body, which was lookt upon to be the immediate

P

Occasion of his Death; the fourth Wound was on the outside of his Left Leg. My Ld Mohun receiv'd a very large Wound in his Groin; another on the Right Side through his Body, up to the Hilt of his Sword; and the third in his Arm; and other Wounds. As to the further Particulars, we shall refer them to our next.

IV. *The Post Boy*, November 18–20, 1712

London, Nov. 20. A farther account of the Duel fought between his Grace the Duke of Hamilton and the Lord Mohun, is as followeth:

Major-General Mackartney went Three times to the Duke's House with a Challenge from the Lord Mohun; on Friday last at Four in the Afternoon he deliver'd it to the Duke, and was at the Bagnio all Night with my Lord Mohun, who was observ'd to be seiz'd with Fear and Trembling at that time. They met at 7 the next Morning, with their Seconds, Col. Hamilton of the Foot-Guards for the Duke, and Mackartney for the Lord Mohun; there the Duke told Mackartney, That his Grace knew this was all of his Contrivance, but that he should have a Share in the Dance; for his Friend Hamilton resolv'd to entertain him. On Tuesday last, a Committee of Council sate at the Earl of Dartmouth's Office, and the Spectators of the Duel were examin'd, and we hear, that my Lord Duke and the Lord Mohun did not parry, but gave Thrusts at each other; and the latter shortening his Sword, stabb'd the Duke in the upper part of his Left Breast, running downwards into his Body, (which Wound, upon probing, was about 14 Inches long) who expired soon after he was put into the Coach. Col. Hamilton receiv'd a Wound in his Right Leg; and going afterwards to the Half-Moon Tavern in Cheapside, was dress'd by Mr. Woodward the Chirurgeon. His Grace is universally lamented by all Men of Honour and Honesty, or who have the least Regard for their Queen and Country; being a faithful Subject, a true Friend, a kind Master, and a loving Husband; And as a just Reward for his Services and Sufferings, was preferr'd to the greatest Honours and Employments of the Crown. His Grace is succeeded in Honour and Estate by his eldest Son, who is about 12 Years of Age. It is to be remembred that the Lord Mohun was the Person who gave the Affront, which the Duke, observing him to be in Drink, disdain'd to regard. But the Faction, weary of him, resolv'd to employ him in some real Service to their Cause, and valu'd not what came of him, provided he did their Drudgery. For the Dispute at Law between the Duke and his Lordship had continu'd many Years, without any personal Quarrel of Consequence. But this is the new Expedient of the Faction, Band-boxes and B(u)llies. Mackartney is absconded, but 'tis hop'd a Proclamation will soon be issu'd out for apprehending him, in order to bring him to Justice. N.B. This is the 4th Person that my Lord Mohun had the Misfortune to kill. His Lordship's Title is extinct.

THE PROCLAMATION

The Post Boy, January 1–3, 1712–13

Whereas by an Inquisition taken the 17th day of November last, upon View of the dead Body of JAMES Duke of HAMILTON and BRANDON, it was found that Gen. Mackartney, Esq.; was aiding and assisting the Lord Mohun to commit the murder on the said Duke; and that the said Mackartney is fled for the same: And whereas it hath since appear'd upon Oath, That the Wound whereof the said Duke died, was given him by the said Mackartney; And Her Majesty having been graciously pleased to issue out Her Royal Proclamation, for apprehending the said Mackartney, promising a Reward of Five Hundred Pounds to such Persons as shall apprehend him; Her Grace the Duchess of HAMILTON and BRANDON, doth hereby promise, That whosoever shall discover the said George Mackartney, so that he may be apprehended, and brought to Justice, shall receive from her Grace a Reward of Three Hundred Pounds, over and above what is promis'd by Her Majesty; to be paid by the Right Honour. Sir Richard Hoare, Knt. Lord Mayor of this City.

V. *The Post Boy*, January 27–29, 1712–13

London, Jan. 29

A Report having been industriously spread, That Mr. Skelton, a Gentleman lately come from France, by Licence from Her Majesty, under Her Privy-Seal, intending a Visit to Mr. Lewis, the Earl of Dartmouth's Secretary, to thank him for the Dispatch of the said Licence, went by mistake to one Mr. Henry Lewis in Marlborough-street, and told him he had Services to him from the Lords Perth and Melfort. These are to satisfy the Publick, That the said Mr. Henry Lewis declar'd yesterday before the Lords of the Cabinet Council, as he had likewise done before in Presence of the Earl of Peterborow, and several Gentlemen, That the said Report was utterly False.

Her MAJESTIE'S
most Gracious SPEECH
to both Houses of Parliament
on Thursday
the Ninth Day of April, 1713

My Lords and Gentlemen,

I Ended the last Session with My hearty Thanks for the Solemn Assurances you had given me, by which I have been Enabled to overcome the Difficulties contriv'd to Obstruct the General Peace.

I have deferred Opening the Session until now, being Desirous to Communicate to you, at your first Meeting, the Success of this Important Affair; It is therefore with great Pleasure I tell you the Treaty is Signed, and in a few Days the Ratifications will be Exchanged.

The Negotiation has been Drawn into so great a Length, that all Our Allies have had sufficient Opportunity to Adjust their several Interests, though the Publick Charge has been thereby much encreased; yet I hope My People will be easie under it, since We have happily obtain'd the End We propos'd.

What I have done for Securing the Protestant Succession, and the perfect Friendship there is between Me and the House of *Hanover,* may Convince such who Wish well to Both, and Desire the Quiet and Safety of their Country, how vain all Attempts are to Divide Us, and those who would make a Merit by Separating Our Interests, will never attain their ill Ends.

Gentlemen of the House of Commons,

As great a Progress has been made in Reducing the Publick Expence, as the Circumstances of Affairs would admit.

What Force may be necessary for Securing Our Commerce by Sea, and for Guards and Garisons, I leave entirely to My Parliament.

Make your selves Safe, and I shall be Satisfied.

Next to the Protection of the Divine Providence, I Depend upon the Loyalty and Affection of My People.

I want no other Guarranty.

I Recommend to your Care those Brave Men who have served well by Sea or Land this War, and cannot be Imploy'd in time of Peace.

I must desire you to provide the Supplies you shall judge requisite, and to give such Dispatch as may be necessary for your own Ease and the Publick Service.

My Lords and Gentlemen,

The many Advantages I have obtain'd for My own Subjects, have occasioned much Opposition, and long Delay to this Peace.

It affords Me great Satisfaction, that My People will have it in their Power, by Degrees, to repair what they have suffered during so long and burdensom a War.

The Easing Our Foreign Trade, as far as is consistent with National Credit, will deserve your Care.

And to think of proper Methods for improving and encouraging Our Home Trade and Manufactures, particularly the Fishery, which may be carry'd on to employ all Our spare Hands, and be a mighty Benefit even to the remotest Parts of this Kingdom.

Several Matters were laid before you last Session, which the Weight and Multiplicity of other Business would not permit you to perfect; I hope you will take a proper Opportunity to give them due Consideration.

I cannot however but expresly mention My Displeasure

at the Unparallel'd Licentiousness in publishing Seditious and Scandalous Libels.

The Impunity such Practices have met with, has encourag'd the Blaspheming every Thing Sacred, and the Propagating Opinions tending to the Overthrow of all Religion and Government.

Prosecutions have been order'd, but it will require some New Law to put a Stop to this growing Evil, and your best Endeavours in your respective Stations to Discourage it.

The Impious Practice of Duelling requires some speedy and effectual Remedy.

Now we are entring upon Peace Abroad, let Me Conjure you all to use your utmost Endeavours for Calming Mens Minds at Home, That the Arts of Peace may be Cultivated.

Let not groundless Jealousies, contriv'd by a Faction, and fomented by Party-Rage, effect that which Our Foreign Enemies could not.

I pray God to direct all your Consultations for His Glory and the Welfare of My People.

FINIS.

TEXTUAL NOTES

1. THE|*CONDUCT*|OF THE|ALLIES,|AND OF THE|𝕷𝖆𝖙𝖊 𝕸𝖎𝖓𝖎𝖘𝖙𝖗𝖞,|IN|Beginning and Carrying on|THE|P r e s e n t W a r.|(Double Rule)|—*Partem tibi Gallia nostri*|*Eripuit: partem duris Hispania bellis:*|*Pars jacet Hesperia: totoq; exercitus orbe*|*Te vincente perit*——|*Odimus accipitrem quia semper vivit in armis.*|——*Victrix Provincia plorat.*|(Double Rule.)|LONDON,|Printed for *John Morphew*, near *Statio-*|*ners-Hall.* 1712. Published November 27, 1711.

2. Same title, except that single rules are substituted before and after the quotation, to allow for the addition of two lines after *perit*: *Terris fudisse cruorem*|*Quid juvat Arctois, Rhodano, Rhenoq; subactis?* and the further addition, between rules, of **The Second Edition, Corrected.** The date is changed to 1711. Published November 29, 1711.

3. Same title, except for the change to **The Third Edition, Corrected.** Published December 3, 1711.

4. For facsimile of title, see page 3. Published December 5, 1711.

Swift clearly states that this was the last edition for which he was himself responsible: 'I stopt the Second Edition, and made all possible Enquiries among those who I thought could best inform me, in order to correct any Error I could hear of; I did the same to the Third and Fourth Editions, and then left the Printer to his Liberty.' See above, p. 96.

I have therefore used for my text an uncut copy of this edition in the Yale Library, and give below a list of variants in the earlier editions. This indicates all corrections of misprints I have made in my text. I have also added variants from the first Dublin edition printed by Hyde in 1712, and in Faulkner's reprint in the *Works*, Vol. V, which shows that Swift or some of his friends made further verbal changes.

After the fourth edition, the printer was allowed to make cheaper reprints in smaller type with half the number of sheets; but though they still carry the words *corrected edition*, this was merely in imitation of the title-page of the fourth. The fifth edition appeared on December 18, 'in small, and sold for sixpence, three times the size of the usual edition (4000).' On January 28, Swift reports in the *Journal to Stella* the sixth edition is sold, and the printer talks of a seventh. At that time 11,000 copies had been sold. Three editions had also appeared in Ireland, and one in Edinburgh 'Reprinted by Mr. Robert Freebairn, and sold at his Shop in the Parliament-Close, 1712.'

An eighth edition, an exact reprint of the seventh, was published in 1715.

Page	Line	PRESENT TEXT	VARIANTS
5	8	*Person*	*Man* 1, H, F
7	13	undertaken	undertakes (*misprint in* 4)
8	2 f.b.	behoves	behooves 1
9	22	both sides 1, 6, 7, H, F	both 2, 3, 4
11	10	of a Peace	of Peace H, F
	25	the present	this 1, H, F,
	28	the Earl of *Godolphin* G——*n*, 3, 4	a certain *Great Person* 1, 2, H, F
	5 f.b.	Lord High Treasurer	at the Head of the Treasury 1, 2, H, F

Q

Page	Line	Present Text	Variants
13	1	being then willing	being willing, H, F
	28	Royal Highness	Highness 1, H, F
14	1	Subsidies 1, H, F	Subsides (*misprint in* 2, 3, 4)
	14	We rightly thought	we thought 1, 2, H, F
	20	but, if	but, that if 1, H, F
	8 f.b.	become 1, H, F	became (*misprint in* 2, 3, 4)
15	5	the Year 1688?	1688? 1, H, F
16	3	our Selves	our Allies (*misprint in* 2)
19	4 f.b.	go on with	continue 1, H, F
22	12	Heads 1, H, F	Hands (*misprint in* 2, 3, 4)
	4 f.b.	took 1, H, F	tooke (*misprint in* 2, 3, 4)
24	15	hardly	not H, F
25	14	We also are	We are also 1, H, F
	l.line	were wiser	are wiser H, F
27	25 ff.	however our Posterity may hereafter, by the Tyranny and Oppression of any succeeding Princes, be reduced to the fatal Necessity of breaking in upon the excellent and happy Settlement now in force.	how much soever the Necessities of the Kingdom may require it. 1, 2, 3, H, F
29	20	Favourites	Favourers H
30	*last* 8 ll.	The Troops we maintain in *Flanders* . . . upwards of sixty thousand:	*Omitted in* 1, 2, 3, H, F
31	1-2	And it is well known, that the Battles of *Hochstet* and *Ramellies* were fought with not above fifty thousand Men on a side.	*Omitted in* 1, H, F
32	*last* 7 ll. &	I shall add one Example	*Omitted in* 1, H, F
33	1-6	more, . . . and would not recal his Grant	
34	8 f.b.	in Employment	in Business 1, 2, 3, H, F
36	2	Matter	Matetr (*misprint in* 3, 4)

N.B.—It is strange that the same misprint is repeated from ed. 3. But as these pages are set line for line, it looks as though the additions to the '4th ed. corrected' were made without completely resetting the type.

39	4 f.b.	could spare	could possibly spare 1, 2, H, F
40	17	owing to the	owing to to the (*misprint in* 3, 4)
	6 f.b.	my Lord *Godolphin*	a certain *Great Man* 1, H, F
41	8 f.b.	unmeasurable Love	unanswerable Love 1, H
43	28	Opportunity, which	Opportunity that fell, which 1, H, F
	33	*wexed*	*waxed* 1, H, F
44	26	*It is better to dwell in a corner of the Housetop, than with a brawling Woman in a wide House.*	*It is better to live on the House Tops, than with a scolding Woman in a large House.* 1, 2, H, F.

Page	Line	PRESENT TEXT	VARIANTS
49	9 f.b.	Preliminary Articles	Articles in that Treaty 1, H, F
51	22	Posture (Po-|sture)	Po,| sture (*misprint in* 2, 3, 4)
	f.n.	*We and* Holland ... *Monarchy*	*Omitted in* 1, H, F
54	22	lasts	lasted H; be to last F
58	12	*strong Delusion*	strong Delusion 1, H, F
60	9 f.b.	For an absolute Government may endure a long War, but it hath generally been ruinous to Free Countries.	*Omitted in* 1 H, F
63	6	were made	were given 1, H, F
64	15	would desire	desire 1, H, F

The above variants indicate quite definitely that Faulkner must have used for his text of Vol. V a copy of the Dublin edition printed from the 1st London edition in 1712.

The title page is an exact reprint of the first edition with the change in imprint only, viz.:

DUBLIN,\|Re-Printed for *John Hyde* Bookseller\|in *Dames.street.* 1712

Faulkner's text does not therefore include the corrections and important additions which Swift had himself carefully made in the later London editions, so that it seemed to me I had no choice but to print from the fourth of these editions after which he says he left it in the hands of the printer. Nevertheless, when Faulkner's text is compared with Hyde's, there are a number of variants which must have been made by someone, when Vol. V was in proof. Faulkner himself states that Swift had the proofs of both Vols. V and VI read to him, and himself made corrections. And this may well have been so. Swift clearly did not bother to see that the text used was the one he had finally approved, but it may still be as Faulkner claimed that he did take the trouble to make some improvements for the sake of greater clarity while the book was still in proof. Some of these variants are, however, more likely to have been introduced in Faulkner's shop, such changes as *although* for *though, It is* for *'Tis,* and perhaps, too, some rather pedantic changes of tense. Nevertheless, it seems worth while to list all the variants (ignoring changes of punctuation, capitalization and spelling) as it is entirely possible that Swift may have been responsible for some of them. Who else but Swift, for instance, would be likely to have changed this remark:

hardly one in five hundred are in the *Pretender*'s Interest

to read

'one in five thousand'?

And he may well have added the names inserted as footnotes.

Page	Line	PRESENT TEXT	FAULKNER, VOL. V
6	13	*Years War*	*Years Wars*
	16	*suspecting, we*	*suspecting that we*
8	13	though	although (*passim*)
	6 f.b.	'Tis	It is

Page	Line	PRESENT TEXT	FAULKNER, VOL. V
9	9	transports	transport
	10	of this	from this
	6*f.b.*	our own Continent	our Continent
	2*f.b.*	latter	later
10	13	an Alliance	Alliance
	25	The Person	The *Person

Fn. *Doctor* Burnet, *Bishop of* Sarum.

	3*f.b.*	that might in	that in
11	13	by the	with the
	28	the Earl of *Godolphin*	a certain *Great Person*

Fn. *Earl of* Godolphin.

	3*f.b.*	of *One*	of *One*

Fn. *Duke of* Marlborough.

12	24	Country	County
14	3	their Troops	the Troops
	12	Aversion for	Aversion from
16	1	beginning of it	beginning it
18	4	Principal	Parties
	29	begun	began
19	4	That	I say, that
	14	War	Wars
	16	so easy	being so easy
20	5	Successes	Success
	18	to the determining	to determine
	7*f.b.*	exhausting all our	exhausting our
21	23	only General	only *General

Fn. *The Earl of* Peterborough, *lately deceased.*

	25	the Kingdom	that Kingdom
25	1	yet here	yet there
	8	who were	who are
	21	thinks	think
27	1-2	acknowledges . . . promises	hath acknowledged . . . promised
	2	his Dominions	that King's Dominions
	13	one in five hundred	one in five thousand
31	13	of building	for building
32	17	that lies under	that were under
35	27	settled. First, It	settled. It
37	18	own particular Quota	own Quota
39	10	present Lord Treasurer	*present Lord Treasurer

Fn. *Earl of* Oxford.

	19	carry over	carried over
40	28	the People	our People
41	11	Ambition	Power
42	10	several were Persons	several Persons
	14	be the sole	be sole
43	32	So when	Thus when
48	14	as well in	as well as in
49	5	and they	while they
50	8	The Person	*The Person

Fn. *HORATIO* WALPOLE, Secretary to the Embassy.

Page	Line	PRESENT TEXT	FAULKNER, VOL. V
51	2	which ruins	which must have ruined
	6	we had	we have
54	18	would pay Interest for	were sufficient to pay Interest
	22	lasts	be to last
	27	a fourth Part	a sixth Part
55	*last line*	hang up	hung up
56	7	Are not	Is not
	21	used to do	were wont to do
59	27	a Man	a *Man
		*Fn. *The late Lord* Hallifax.	
60	18	it is worth	its worth
63	23	returns and gets	return and get
	28	is ended	be ended
64	2	are forced	be forced

2. SOME ADVICE TO THE MEMBERS OF THE OCTOBER CLUB

First printed January 22, 1711–12. See *Advt.* in The Post Boy, Jan. 20–22, 1711–12. For facsimile of t.p. see p. 69.

Reprinted by Faulkner in *Works*, 1738, Vol. VI, pp. 119–136. Also in *Political Tracts*. By the Author of Gulliver's Travels. Printed for C. Davis in Pater-Noster-Row, 1738, Vol. II, pp. 119–136.

The present text is printed from a photostat of the first edition; and this has been collated with the text of Faulkner.

Page	Line	PRESENT TEXT	FAULKNER
		See Appendix A.	The Preface
71	*h.t.*	SOME|ADVICE, &c.	SOME|ADVICE|HUMBLY OFFERED TO THE| MEMBERS|OF THE| *OCTOBER* CLUB.
	5 f.b.	Counterpart	Counter Part
75	3 f.b.	be effectually removed	effectually be removed
76	*last line*	Scars F	Fears (*Misprint in 1st ed.*)
79	4	that Power	the Power

3. SOME REMARKS ON THE BARRIER TREATY

First printed February 22, 1711–12. See *Advt.* in 'The Supplement' (Morphew) February 20–22, 1711–12. For facsimile of t.p. see p. 83. The so-called second edition is actually set up from the same type; only the t.p. being reset to allow for the addition of THE SECOND EDITION in black letter between rules.

Reprinted by Faulkner in *Works*, 1738, Vol. VI, pp. 345–386. Also in *Political Tracts* By the Author of Gulliver's Travels. Printed for C. Davis in Pater-Noster-Row, 1738, Vol. II, pp. 173–217.

The present text is printed from my own copy of the first edition; and this has been collated with the text of Faulkner.

Page	Line	Present Text	Faulkner
87	10	their stead	his stead
	6 f.b.	*Motives* to	Motives with
90	7 f.b.	Gand	Grand (*misprint*)
92	22	beneficial Bargains	*beneficial Bargains*
	28	*our own Legislature*	*our Legislature*
94	7 f.b.	*are not we*	are we not
96	11	*Loyal Ministry*	and loyal Ministry
98	9	*the said States-Genera*	*the States-General*
	25	*new Wars*	*new War*
	7 f.b.	*of Her*	to Her
	4 f.b.	*the* Sieurs F	*to the Sieurs* (*misprint in* 1)
104	7 f.b.	as favourably as the People the most favoured	as the People the most favoured
106	10	nor formal	or formal
110	7	Attack F	Tack (*misprint in* 1)
111	12	*the Two*	in the two

4. A LETTER TO A WHIG LORD

Title: See facsimile, p. 121.

First printed in June, 1712.

Reprinted in A Supplement to Dr. Swift's Works. London: Printed for F. Cogan, at the Middle Temple Gate, Fleet-street, 1752, pp. 50–70.

The text is printed from a photostat of the copy in the Yale Library, which is identical with the two Bodleian copies. Some corrections were made and some errors introduced into the text of 1752, as indicated by the following variants:

Page	Line	Present Text		Variants	
123	17	thoroughly	52	thoroughly	12
		the only	52	only	12
	19	not aware	12 (*Errata*)	but aware	12, 52
125	7 f.b.	above Twenty	12	about Twenty	52
126	20	Court	12 (*Errata*)	Courts	12, 52
	23	than	12	that	52
	27	than	12	then	52
128	26	even into	12	even in	52
131	29	is cancelled	12	cancelled	52

5. A HUE AND CRY AFTER DISMAL

For facsimile, see Frontispiece.

A half-sheet, printed on one side only, first published July 17, 1712.

The text is printed from the facsimile of the copy in the Bodleian (MSS. Rawl. D 383 (135)) which is identical with the other copy in the possession of Lord Rothschild.

A second edition was issued with a new title and additions, given in the list of variants below. A copy of this is also in the Bodleian (Pamphlets 305 (53)).

	Present Text	Variants
Title:	**A Hue and Cry after Dismal;**	Dunkirk *to be let*, Or, *A Town Ready* Furnish'd |WITH|**A Hue and Cry after Dismal:**

Page	Line		
139	4	*General* Hill.	*General* Hill. *To which is added the Copy of a* PAPER *that was found in his Pocket.*
	5	*at small*	*at a small*
	6	*than to*	*then to*
	12	Bunch	a Bunch
	26	That	This
140	1	Hobb	Stobb (in both editions)

(I can make no sense of 'each Stobb', and have ventured to treat it as a misreading of Swift's capital *H*, which is not unlike *St*.)

| | 6-7 | about him. | about him. It is said, that he had the following Verses found in his Pocket, which he scatter'd up and down the Town. |

> *Old* Lewis *thus the Terms of Peace to Burnish,*
> *Has lately let out* Dunkirk *Ready Furnish'd;*
> *But whether 'tis by* Lease *or* Coppy-hold,
> *Or* Tenure in Capite, *we've not been told*:
> *But this we hope, if yet he pulls his Horns in,*
> *He'll be oblig'd to give his Tenants Warning.*

	19-20	Chimney-Sweeper (though that was too good a Trade for him) but	*Chimney-Sweeper,* but
	23	Pail full	Pail-full
	24	Then they	They then
	26	Labor-in-vain	Labour in vain.
		whispered	whispering
	27	may plainly (2)	planly (*misprint in* 1)
	3-4 f.b.	The Governor then sorry	Then the Governor *very sorry*
141	6	hath been	and hath been
Imprint:		London, Printed in the Year, 1712	LONDON Printed in the YEAR. M.DCCXII.

6. A LETTER FROM THE PRETENDER TO A WHIG LORD

Half-sheet, printed on one side only. No Imprint.
Letter dated S. Germain, July 8, 1712.
First published in July, 1712.
Reprinted in A SUPPLEMENT TO DR. SWIFT'S WORKS, LONDON, PRINTED FOR J. NICHOLS, MDCCLXXIX, p. 163.
The present text is printed from a photostat of the copy in the Lambeth Library.

7. LORD WHARTON'S LETTER TO THE BISHOP OF ST. ASAPH

For facsimile of title, see p. 149.

First printed in July, 1712.

Reprinted in A SUPPLEMENT TO DR. SWIFT'S WORKS, 1779, Vol. XIV, pp. 185–195.

The present text is printed from a photostat of the Harvard copy, which is identical with the copy at Yale and the two Bodleian copies, except that the Godwin copy (Pamphlets 2006 (22)) is lacking the first leaf with the half-title.

8–10. THREE EXAMINERS

The text of these three papers is taken from a photostat of the Yale copy of the original *Examiners*, in folio:

    8. Vol. II, Numb. 34, From Thursday July 17 to July 24, 1712
    9. Vol. III, Numb. 16, From Monday Jan. 12 to Jan. 16, 1712–13
    10. Vol. III, Numb. 21, From Friday Jan. 30 to Feb. 2, 1712–13

Names and titles appearing with initials only have been given in full and misprints have been corrected.

11. THE HUMBLE ADDRESS OF THE LORDS TO HER MAJESTY, 11 April, 1713

For facsimile of the t.p., see p. 181.

The text is printed from a photostat of the Bodleian copy, which has been collated with the photograph of Swift's autograph, preserved in the Portland MSS., Welbeck Abbey, and reproduced here facing page xxviii by the kind permission of the Duke of Portland. Words printed below between square brackets are underscored in the draft.

Page	Line	PRESENT TEXT	*Swift's MS. draft, April* 9
183	11	humble	humblest
	13	Your Parliament . . . Concluded;	this House concluded, [so honorable to Your Majesty and safe and advantageous to Your Kingdoms;]
	15	in few Years	in a few Years
	16	And also do Congratulate Your Majesty upon the Success of Your Endeavours for a General Peace.	[We likewise beg leave to congratulate with Your Majesty upon the generall Peace you have procured for all Your Allyes, wherein the true Interests and just Pretensions of each are so fully provided for that the Tranquility and Welfare of Europe will be owing (next to the Divine Providence) to Your Majesty's Wisdom and Goodness.]
	19	great Support and Ornament	greatest Ornament and Protector
	20	take, as You have always done, the	take the

Page Line	PRESENT TEXT	*Swift's MS. draft, April* 9
23	Friendship (*Harley's correction*)	[Harmony]
25	You Express	You are pleased to express
29	the Dutiful Returns that can be paid, by	Returns that can be due from

APPENDIXES

A. The Publisher's Preface to SOME ADVICE ... TO MEMBERS OF THE OCTOBER CLUB.

The text is printed from Swift's *Works*, printed by G. Faulkner, Dublin 1737, Vol. VI, pp. 121-2.

B. IT'S OUT AT LAST: OR, FRENCH CORRESPONDENCE CLEAR AS THE SUN.

London: Printed in the Year MDCCXII.
Advertised as *Just Published* in THE EXAMINER, July 3-10, 1712.
The text is printed from a photostat of the copy of this half-sheet in the Bodleian (Pamphlets, 305 (50)).

C. *Preface to* FOUR SERMONS ... by William (Fleetwood), Lord Bishop of St. Asaph.

London: Printed for Charles Harper, etc., 1712.
Reprinted in the SPECTATOR for Wed., May 21, 1712.
The text is printed from a photostat of the Bodleian copy (8°. Th. J. 90), pp. iii-xii.

D. Swift's contributions to *The Post Boy* and the *Evening Post* in 1711-1713.

E. HER MAJESTIE'S MOST GRACIOUS SPEECH TO ... PARLIAMENT, April 9, 1713.

London: Printed by John Baskett, etc., MDCCXIII.
The text is printed from a photostat of the Bodleian copy (Vet. A3.c.43).

INDEX